Lecture Notes in Electrical Engineering

Volume 1368

The book series *Lecture Notes in Electrical Engineering* (LNEE) publishes the latest developments in Electrical Engineering—quickly, informally and in high quality. While original research reported in proceedings and monographs has traditionally formed the core of LNEE, we also encourage authors to submit books devoted to supporting student education and professional training in the various fields and applications areas of electrical engineering. The series cover classical and emerging topics concerning:

- Communication Engineering, Information Theory and Networks
- Electronics Engineering and Microelectronics
- Signal, Image and Speech Processing
- Wireless and Mobile Communication
- Circuits and Systems
- Energy Systems, Power Electronics and Electrical Machines
- Electro-optical Engineering
- Instrumentation Engineering
- Avionics Engineering
- Control Systems
- Internet-of-Things and Cybersecurity
- Biomedical Devices, MEMS and NEMS

For general information about this book series, comments or suggestions, please contact leontina.dicecco@springer.com.

To submit a proposal or request further information, please contact the Publishing Editor in your country:

China

Jasmine Dou, Editor (jasmine.dou@springer.com)

India, Japan, Rest of Asia

Swati Meherishi, Editorial Director (Swati.Meherishi@springer.com)

Southeast Asia, Australia, New Zealand

Ramesh Nath Premnath, Editor (ramesh.premnath@springernature.com)

USA, Canada

Michael Luby, Senior Editor (michael.luby@springer.com)

All other Countries

Leontina Di Cecco, Senior Editor (leontina.dicecco@springer.com)

**** This series is indexed by EI Compendex and Scopus databases. ****

G. K. Rajanikant · Pascaline Pré
Editors

Perspectives on Global Transformation

Proceedings of Research Conclave on Global Transformation 2024 (ReCon-GT24)

Springer

Editors
G. K. Rajanikant
Department of Biosciences and Engineering
National Institute of Technology Calicut
Calicut, Kerala, India

Pascaline Pré
Department of Energy Systems
and Environment
IMT Atlantique, Campus de Nantes
Nantes, France

ISSN 1876-1100 ISSN 1876-1119 (electronic)
Lecture Notes in Electrical Engineering
ISBN 978-981-96-6706-2 ISBN 978-981-96-6707-9 (eBook)
https://doi.org/10.1007/978-981-96-6707-9

This Springer imprint is published by the registered company Springer Nature Singapore Pte Ltd.
The registered company address is: 152 Beach Road, #21-01/04 Gateway East, Singapore 189721, Singapore

Overview

Editors: Dr. G. K. Rajanikant, Dr. Pascaline Pré

- Includes proceedings of ReCon-GT24.
- Covers research in the areas of Machine Learning and Artificial Intelligence, Computation and Modelling, Healthcare and Biomedical Applications, Systems and Computing, Theoretical Design and Circular Economy.
- Is a valuable resource for students, academics, and practitioners working on global sustainability challenges.

About This Book

This volume presents a curated collection of peer-reviewed articles from the Research Conclave on Global Transformation 2024 (ReCon-GT24), held on April 19–20, 2024, under the overarching theme of sustainability, inclusivity, and resilience. The book encompasses research spanning a diverse array of topics, including Machine Learning and Artificial Intelligence, Computation and Modelling, Healthcare and Biomedical Applications, Systems and Computing, Theoretical Design and Circular Economy. The contributions featured within this volume are authored by academicians, researchers, and students, thereby reflecting a rich tapestry of perspectives and insights. Furthermore, this compilation explores essential concepts related to interdisciplinary collaboration and innovative strategies aimed at addressing global sustainability challenges. As such, this book serves as a valuable resource for students, academics, and practitioners across various disciplines who are engaged in discussions and initiatives geared toward fostering a more sustainable and inclusive future.

Contents

Integrating Knowledge-Guided Layers with Fine-Tuned VGG-16 for Improved Thyroid Malignancy Classification: Explainability with Grad-CAM 1
Sujithra Sankar and S. Sathyalakshmi

Aroma Detection: A Brief Study on Olfactory Science Using AI 21
Muhammed Mizhab, K. S. Divya, Bovas Eldho, S. Nandana, and V. B. Gowri

Single Channel EEG Classification for Motor Task 29
Joel George, Joel Jose, Lakshmi S. Nair, Sandra Skaria, P. Suresh, and Y. Sheena

Agrobot: An Intelligent Crop Management Robot for Sustainable Crop Production and Precision Farming 43
K. Ankita Shenoy, Anu Yeldho, James Panikulam, Sagar S. Abraham, Angel Varghese, C. V. Priya, and Nivea Kesav

Intelligent Fall Detection Vest with Integrated Airbag System for Elderly Safety 57
Anne Staicy Philip, Albin Sunil Skaria, Angith S. Menon, C. K. Hariprasad, and Reshma Jose

Efficient Maximum and Minimum Finding Circuits for Machine Learning Applications 67
P. Shareefa Fairoose and Ashutosh Mishra

Association Between the Chirality of a Filament and the Helicity of the Supporting Active Regions 73
P. T. Jain Jacob and Ram Ajor Maurya

Investigating Coronal Loop Dynamics: Harmonic Behavior and Magnetic Field Estimation 81
K. Safna Banu and Ram Ajor Maurya

Quasi Periodic Oscillation in a Coronal Mass Ejection Due to Shock Wave ... 89
Sachin Rajkapoor Kanaujiya, Ram Ajor Maurya, and P. T. Jain Jacob

Power and Area Efficient VLSI Algorithms for Auditory Compensation in Digital Hearing Aids ... 95
Ani Abraham, Manju Manuel, and P. G. Geo

Technical and Scale Efficiency of Thermal Power Generation Companies in India: A DEA Approach ... 109
Sayan Chandran and Sunitha Sivaraman

Modeling and Analysis of Pulsed Electric Field Treatment Chambers for Liquid Food Processing ... 123
Gajula Chandanasree, Thomas Mohan, and K. J. Suja

About the Editors

Dr. G. K. Rajanikant is a prominent faculty member at the School of Biosciences and Engineering, NIT Calicut. His work focuses on neuroscience, regenerative biology, neurological disorders, ischemic neuroprotection, and real-time sensor development for neurotransmitter detection. He has an h index of 31, an i10-index of 59, and over 3000 citations, reflecting his impactful contributions to the field. He holds multiple patents, particularly for compositions mimicking the effects of calorie restriction and ischemic preconditioning. His dedication has earned him accolades such as the Stem Cell Society Singapore Fellowship (2018) and the Best Publication Award from the DBT-Bioinformatics Infrastructure Facility (2014). He actively participates in advisory roles and expert committees, including the Programme Advisory Committee of The Kerala State Council for Science, Technology and Environment (KSCSTE), and holds editorial positions in top journals like *PLOS ONE*. Dr. Rajanikant's commitment to fostering scientific collaboration and innovation is evident in his role as an international grant evaluator, reviewer for prestigious publications, and as an organizing chair for key scientific workshops and symposiums.

Dr. Pascaline Pré is a distinguished professor at IMT Atlantique in the Department of Energy Systems and Environment, leading the VERTE research group on energy valorization from residues and gas conditioning. She coordinates the "Energy and Process Engineering" department at Carnot M.I.N.E.S Institute. Her research spans novel adsorbents, transfer-reaction modeling in porous media, and developing processes for green gas production, energy storage, and pollutant capture. Since 2018, Pascaline has overseen the Energy and Process Engineering department and served on the French Association of Adsorption (AFA) board. She co-leads the "EnergICs" national program and has been active in the Erasmus Mundus ME3 Master's course. With 16 supervised doctoral theses and numerous publications, her research is widely recognized (H-index 17,900+ citations). She also contributes to industry initiatives and serves as an expert for HCERES and the EMC2 cluster. Committed to gender equity, Dr. Pascaline has led equity initiatives at IMT Atlantique since 2019, driving sustainable and energy-efficient research and education programs.

Integrating Knowledge-Guided Layers with Fine-Tuned VGG-16 for Improved Thyroid Malignancy Classification: Explainability with Grad-CAM

Sujithra Sankar and S. Sathyalakshmi

Abstract Background: Thyroid cancer presents a significant global health challenge, necessitating precise and timely interventions. Several recent studies have used transfer learning techniques for thyroid cancer classification from ultrasound images. While existing research has achieved promising results using transfer learning for thyroid cancer classification from ultrasound images, two key limitations remain unaddressed: Use of domain knowledge, and Explainability. Existing state-of-the-art deep learning models fail to leverage domain knowledge effectively. Aim: This work addresses this gap by proposing a novel explainable deep learning architecture incorporating domain knowledge. The proposed model incorporates feature extraction by VGG-16 convolutional layers, a domain-specific knowledge block, and a classification network for accurate malignancy classification. A Gradient-weighted Class Activation Mapping (Grad-CAM), integrated with our model, is an explainability tool. Method: The proposed customised knowledge-guided block is tailored based on the importance of high-ranked features such as composition, echogenicity, shape, margins, and calcifications. The 18-layer architecture includes 13 convolutional layers of the VGG-16 base model for feature extraction, 1 layer in domain knowledge-guided block, 1 concatenation and flattening layer, and 3 dense classification layers for accurate classification of thyroid ultrasound images. Results: Our approach achieves state-of-the-art predictive performance, with an accuracy of 92.84%. Grad-CAM generates heatmaps highlighting regions and features in ultrasound images crucial for cancer classification. By incorporating domain knowledge into deep learning architecture, we enable its effective application in real-world clinical settings, specifically for the classification of thyroid cancer. Our approach achieves state-of-the-art accuracy, while Grad-CAM empowers clinicians to understand the model's reasoning.

S. Sankar (✉)
Department of Computer Applications, Muthoot Institute of Technology and Science, Kochi, Kerala, India
e-mail: sujithra.sankar@gmail.com

S. Sathyalakshmi
Department of Computer Science and Engineering, Hindustan Institute of Technology and Science, Chennai, Tamil Nadu, India

G. K. Rajanikant and P. Pré (eds.), *Perspectives on Global Transformation*, Lecture Notes in Electrical Engineering 1368, https://doi.org/10.1007/978-981-96-6707-9_1

Keywords Transfer learning · VGG-16 · Thyroid cancer · Grad-CAM · Classification and prediction · Explainability

1 Introduction

The American Cancer Society Cancer Statistics Centre [1] projects over 2 million new cases of thyroid cancer in 2024, with an estimated 611,720 deaths. In thyroid cancer prediction, transfer learning techniques have gained popularity as an effective approach for overcoming challenges related to limited labeled data and computational constraints. Transfer learning leverages the knowledge of pre-trained models on large datasets, adapting it for specific medical imaging tasks. This paper explores the use of the VGG-16 transfer learning model [2] for thyroid cancer prediction, uncovering complex relationships between image features and predictions. Through experimentation and validation, this study presents a robust and transparent approach to thyroid cancer prediction.

1.1 Thyroid Cancer Prediction with Transfer Learning Models

The thyroid, a butterfly-shaped gland situated at the neck's base, is a vital regulator of essential bodily functions via thyroid hormone secretion, including thyroxine (T4) and triiodothyronine (T3), crucial for metabolic control. These hormones influence cellular energy usage, temperature regulation, heart rate maintenance, and other critical processes. Thyroid cancer emerges from unchecked growth of abnormal thyroid cells, representing the most prevalent endocrine malignancy with distinct subtypes like papillary, follicular, medullary, and anaplastic thyroid cancer. Despite the benign nature of most thyroid nodules, early identification of malignancy is most crucial in effective treatment.

Deep learning models can analyse thyroid ultrasound images to predict the likelihood of malignancy with high accuracy. These models can augment traditional diagnostic methods like biopsies and fine-needle aspirations. They can offer non-invasive, faster, and less expensive alternatives for initial screening or even risk stratification. Given the asymptomatic nature of early-stage thyroid cancer, accurate predictive models, often using deep learning algorithms like the VGG-16 network for feature extraction, play a crucial role in early detection.

1.2 Deep Learning Models and Explainability

The interpretability of AI models has emerged as a crucial consideration in recent years, especially in scenarios where model decisions have a direct impact on human lives and well-being. Grad-CAM, or Gradient-weighted Class Activation Mapping, operates as a visualisation technique [3], highlighting the regions of an input that are crucial for a model's decision-making.

By using the gradient information flowing through the network during the inference process, Grad-CAM generates heatmaps that highlight the specific locations in the ultrasound image that significantly influence the model's classification and prediction process. For thyroid cancer prediction, this means that medical practitioners and researchers can rely on the model's predictive accuracy and gain insight into the "why?" part of a prediction. This aids in building trust in the model's decisions and provides valuable input for medical professionals in arriving at an explainable diagnosis. The transfer learning capabilities of VGG-16 facilitate high predictive accuracy and Grad-CAM empowers medical professionals with insights into the process of predictions.

1.3 Novelty: Domain Knowledge-Guided Model Integrated with Explainability

Current machine learning methods face limitations as they often overlook essential domain knowledge specific to nodule diagnosis, and thereby diminishing their overall performance. Our proposed model has 18 layers including the base model of VGG-16, which is used as a feature extractor. The proposed deep-learning-based CAD system is guided by domain-specific prior knowledge, for nodule classification and prediction in ultrasound images.

The knowledge-guided block integrates diagnosis-oriented features, in which each feature vector is used to capture and enhance one specific characteristic feature in the thyroid nodule ultrasound image. The proposed model uses VGG-16, a pre-trained model with 16 layers. The proposed architecture integrates the 13 layers (5 blocks of conv2 base layers) of VGG-16 with a knowledge-guided block followed by concatenation and dense fully connected deep neural network layers. In the proposed model, fine-tuned VGG-16 is used. Features such as Composition, Echogenicity, Shape, Margins, and calcifications which are high-ranked features in Thyroid Imaging Reporting and Data System (TI-RADS) scoring, are used in the domain knowledge guided block. Since the VGG-16 model is trained on millions of images of the ImageNet dataset, it facilitates high predictive accuracy. Grad-CAM empowers medical professionals with insights into the process of predictions. By enhancing the accuracy and interpretability of machine learning model predictions, our proposed model aims to improve the prognosis and management of thyroid cancer.

2 Related Work

Both Machine Learning (ML) and Deep Learning (DL) are subfields of Artificial Intelligence (AI) with immense potential in healthcare. They can analyse large datasets of medical images, patient records, and other clinical data to identify patterns and make predictions.

2.1 *Deep Learning Models in Thyroid Disease Predictions*

Numerous research studies have explored the application of Convolutional Neural Networks (CNN) in classifying thyroid cancer ultrasound images. An investigation, led by Zhu et al. [4], introduced a comprehensive Deep Convolutional Neural Network (DCNN) architecture incorporating transfer learning for diagnosing thyroid cancer through ultrasonographic images. Their approach yielded an average classification accuracy of 86.5%.

Recurrent Neural Network (RNN), another influential deep learning technique primarily employed in time-series analysis, has shown promise in cancer diagnosis. A 2022 study by Gayathry et al. [5] proposed an RNN-based model. Their hybrid optimisation approach aims to leverage multispectral photoacoustic imaging and transfer learning techniques to detect and classify cancer using ultrasound images. Notably, this model exhibited outstanding accuracy, surpassing 90%.

In a 2021 investigation led by Li et al. [6], a classification network named CNN-F, incorporating the fusion of low-level and high-level features, was introduced for distinguishing between benign and malignant nodules. The classification accuracy of this network in diagnosing thyroid diseases reached 85.92%.

2.2 *Explainability and Thyroid Clinical Decision Support Systems*

Post hoc methods encompass techniques like Class Activation Mapping (CAM) [7] and Gradient-weighted Class Activation Mapping (Grad-CAM) [8].

In a study conducted in 2023 by Zhao et al. [9], the researchers focused on SPECT thyroid images. The researchers used Grad-CAM to visualise class-specific attentional regions with attention heatmaps. All four pre-trained neural networks demonstrated an overall accuracy exceeding 0.85 for the classification of SPECT thyroid images.

In a 2023 study, Choudhury et al. [10] introduced a framework for interpretable classification of thyroid nodule malignancy. Their approach utilized deep learning to predict binary attributes from ultrasound images and employed Class Activation Mapping (CAM) to highlight the image regions critical for predicting these attributes. Their model achieved a 72% accuracy in distinguishing benign from malignant thyroid nodules. In another 2023 study, Song et al. [11] developed an explainer for classifying benign and malignant cases, which proved to be more effective than Grad-CAM in identifying regions linked to relevant features.

3 Materials and Methods

3.1 Dataset Characteristics

The dataset utilised in this study is the TDID dataset [12], a publicly available resource containing ultrasound (US) images in JPEG format along with ground truth information in XML format, carefully annotated by expert radiologists. Created by the Universidad Nacional de Colombia, the TDID US image dataset includes 380 thyroid cancer cases, with each case consisting of one or more image files. In total, the dataset comprises 455 image files, each in RGB format with a resolution of 560 × 360 pixels. The accompanying XML files provide detailed patient information, including case number, image number, gender, and age, along with nodule characteristics such as composition, echogenicity, margins, and calcifications. Additionally, the XML files contain TI-RADS scores and location coordinates to identify the Region of Interest (RoI) of the nodules in the ultrasound images. The XML file is converted to csv format and the domain values are used in the knowledge guided layers of the model.

The csv file has the attributes case number, age, sex, composition, echogenicity, margins, calcifications, TIRADS, width, heigh, and length to width ratio. The attributes width, height, long to short ratio and taller than wide are calculated attributes using the annotation information of the nodule provided in the XML file. The structure of XML annotation file of the thyroid ultrasound images is shown in Fig. 1, and the structure of csv dataset extracted from XML annotation file is shown in Fig. 2. The case number 4 can be seen as an entry in the csv file.

3.2 The TIRADS Scoring System

The TI-RADS scoring system, developed by the American College of Radiology (ACR) in 2017 [13], seeks to improve diagnostic accuracy while minimising unnecessary biopsies of benign nodules. The TI-RADS scoring scale ranges from 2 to 5, with scores of 2 and 3 categorised as benign, whereas scores of 4a, 4b, 4c, and 5 suggest thyroid malignancy. According to input from radiologists, endocrinologists, and oncologists, thyroid nodule malignancy is typically assessed using the TI-RADS score [14]. The system evaluates five ultrasound features—composition, echogenicity (brightness of the nodule), shape, margin, and punctate echogenic foci (small bright spots indicating calcification). A score is assigned to each feature, and

```
▼<case>
   <number>4</number>
   <age>37</age>
   <sex>F</sex>
   <composition>spongiform</composition>
   <echogenicity>isoechogenicity</echogenicity>
   <margins>well defined</margins>
   <calcifications>microcalcifications</calcifications>
   <tirads>4a</tirads>
   <reportbacaf/>
   <reporteco/>
 ▼<mark>
     <image>1</image>
     <svg>[{"points": [{"x": 366, "y": 175}, {"x": 376, "y": 172}, {"x": 382, "y": 172}, {"x"
     "y": 148}, {"x": 416, "y": 141}, {"x": 418, "y": 137}, {"x": 419, "y": 130}, {"x": 414,
     {"x": 388, "y": 113}, {"x": 384, "y": 112}, {"x": 376, "y": 106}, {"x": 372, "y": 102},
     "y": 91}, {"x": 347, "y": 82}, {"x": 338, "y": 79}, {"x": 329, "y": 79}, {"x": 321, "y":
     295, "y": 70}, {"x": 276, "y": 70}, {"x": 229, "y": 85}, {"x": 221, "y": 88}, {"x": 217,
     {"x": 187, "y": 110}, {"x": 180, "y": 112}, {"x": 175, "y": 117}, {"x": 171, "y": 120},
     "y": 142}, {"x": 159, "y": 147}, {"x": 159, "y": 157}, {"x": 160, "y": 161}, {"x": 162,
     {"x": 186, "y": 192}, {"x": 190, "y": 197}, {"x": 196, "y": 201}, {"x": 199, "y": 204},
     "y": 212}, {"x": 237, "y": 217}, {"x": 275, "y": 220}, {"x": 281, "y": 220}, {"x": 306,
     {"x": 336, "y": 201}, {"x": 343, "y": 196}, {"x": 358, "y": 194}, {"x": 361, "y": 188},
     "y": 175}], "annotation": {}, "regionType": "freehand"}]</svg>
   </mark>
</case>
```


Fig. 1 The structure of XML annotation file of the thyroid ultrasound images

Case No	Age	Sex	Composition	Echogenicity	Margins	Calcifications	TIRADS	width	height	Long_Short_Ratio	taller_than_wide
2	49	F	solid	hyperechogenicity	well defined	non	2	176	224	0.79	0
3	31	F	spongiform	isoechogenicity	well defined	microcalcifications	4a	80	121	0.66	0
4	37	F	spongiform	isoechogenicity	well defined	microcalcifications	4a	150	260	0.58	0
5	47	F	solid	hypoechogenicity	ill defined	microcalcifications	5	128	124	1.03	1
10	74	F	solid	hyperechogenicity	spiculated	microcalcifications	4b	94	115	0.82	0
10	74	F	solid	hyperechogenicity	spiculated	microcalcifications	4b	94	115	0.82	0
10	74	F	solid	hyperechogenicity	spiculated	microcalcifications	4b	94	115	0.82	0
10	74	F	solid	hyperechogenicity	spiculated	microcalcifications	4b	94	115	0.82	0
11	30	F	solid	marked hypoechoge	spiculated	microcalcifications	5	103	105	0.98	0
11	30	F	solid	marked hypoechoge	spiculated	microcalcifications	5	103	105	0.98	0
11	30	F	solid	marked hypoechoge	spiculated	microcalcifications	5	103	105	0.98	0
11	30	F	solid	marked hypoechoge	spiculated	microcalcifications	5	103	105	0.98	0
12	45	F	predominantly s	isoechogenicity	well defined	microcalcifications	4a	100	149	0.67	0
12	45	F	predominantly s	isoechogenicity	well defined	microcalcifications	4a	100	149	0.67	0
12	45	F	predominantly s	isoechogenicity	well defined	microcalcifications	4a	100	149	0.67	0

Fig. 2 The structure of csv dataset extracted from XML annotation file. The case number 4 can be seen as an entry in the csv file

the sum of these scores defines the TI-RADS category and its recommended actions. TI-RADS level 2 suggests a non-suspicious nodule, while level 3 indicates mild suspicion. A score between 4 and 6 results in level 4, reflecting moderate suspicion, whereas 7 or more points signify a TI-RADS level 5, suggesting high suspicion or a potentially malignant nodule. Nodules smaller than 5 mm generally do not require follow-up, even if classified as level 5, as their likelihood of developing into high-risk malignancies is minimal.

3.3 *Our Proposed Knowledge-Guided Deep Learning Architecture*

The proposed model has a core of VGG-16 pre-trained model for the computer vision task as a feature extractor; these extracted features are the input into domain-specific knowledge-guided block. The knowledge-guided block comprises a concatenation layer. Three fully connected dense neural networks are used in the classification and prediction layer. An embedded explainability branch with Grad-CAM is used in interpreting the AI model. Our proposed detection model is comprised of five different phases, and a total of 18 layers including the initial 13 convolutional layers of VGG-16 base model. The proposed model is shown in Fig. 3.

In phase 1, our proposed model extracts features and generates feature maps through the initial 13 convolutional layers of the VGG-16 pre-trained model. The 3 convolutional layers in the 5th block of VGG-16 model are unfrozen and trained.

In phase 2, the extracted feature maps enter the domain knowledge-based block. Feature vectors are created corresponding to the five ultrasound feature values mentioned in Sect. 3.2 in TI-RADS level calculation for thyroid malignancy. In this phase, the feature value of each feature of the image is used in creating the embedded vector for the feature. These embedded dominant attribute vectors are concatenated with the feature maps.

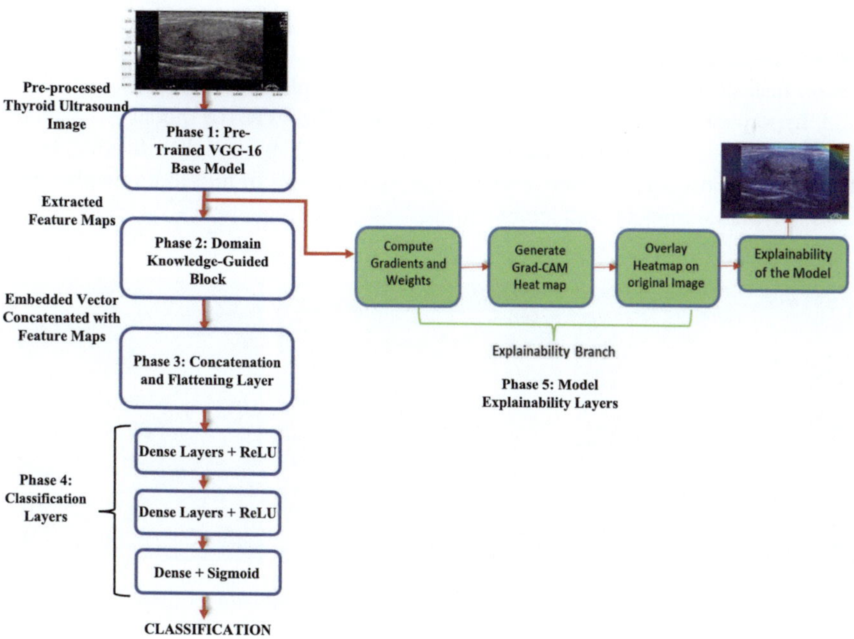

Fig. 3 The architecture of our thyroid malignancy prediction model with embedded Grad-CAM

In phase 3, the concatenated feature maps embedded with the feature vectors enter the concatenation and flattening layer where the feature maps are converted from 2D arrays into a single 1D vector to feed the fully connected layers for classification.

In phase 4, from the concatenation and flattening layer, the output flows into three fully connected dense layers used for classification and prediction. The last dense layer is a sigmoid layer for binary classification and prediction.

In phase 5, from the feature extraction layer, gradient information flowing through the network generates Grad-CAM heatmap. Thus, Grad-CAM serves as a powerful explainability tool in the domain of thyroid ultrasound-based cancer prediction, facilitating the predictive capabilities of deep learning models and the interpretability required for clinical decision-making.

Data Pre-processing. Thyroid ultrasound images undergo preprocessing utilising the annotation details from the XML files in the TDID dataset. Corresponding to each image file, the XML file offers x, y coordinates of the ground truth, guiding the segmentation and cropping of images around the Region of Interest (RoI). This helps diminish unnecessary background noise. To augment the dataset, image manipulation techniques such as flipping, rotating, translating, zooming, and shifting are employed, significantly increasing thc number of images. Before model training, the image size is reduced. These preprocessing steps play a pivotal role in enhancing the cfficiency of deep learning models. Figure 4a, b, and c illustrate the original ultrasound thyroid nodule image alongside its preprocessed versions.

The VGG-16 Transfer Learning Model. Several ablation studies are conducted on VGG-16, Inception-v3 model, Densenet-201, and CNN model for the classification task on thyroid ultrasound images with multiple combinations of architecture, hyperparameters, and optimisation methods. The VGG-16 model consistently demonstrated commendable accuracy in thyroid malignancy classification tasks, displaying robust performance with diverse combinations of fine-tuning with conv2 layers, hyperparameters, and architectures.

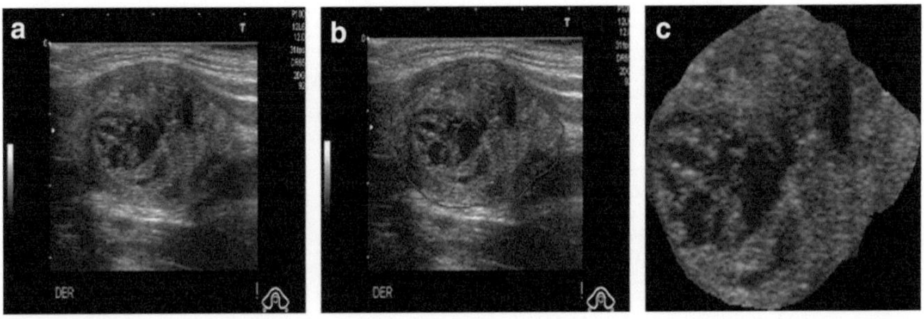

Fig. 4 **a** Thyroid Ultrasound original image, **b** Region of Interest (RoI) outlined in the thyroid ultrasound image and **c** The image segmented along the RoI

VGG-16 serves as a popular backbone for feature extraction in computer vision applications. It is structured with sequential convolutional layers, periodically interrupted by max-pooling layers, and finalised with fully connected layers. The VGG-16 architecture is illustrated in Fig. 5.

Domain Knowledge-Guided Block. The novelty of our proposed architecture lies in the knowledge-guided block that is connected to the fine-tuned VGG-16 base model. Feature maps are extracted from the image using VGG-16 convolutional layers. The five primary features indicative of thyroid malignancy are embedded in vector format. These key features, which are described in detail in Sect. 3.2, are integrated with the feature maps at the concatenation layer. During model training, the network learns to link these features in the ultrasound images with the corresponding features in the vector. Figure 6 provides a comprehensive overview of the domain knowledge-guided block using transfer learning.

Concatenation and Flattening Layers. The concatenation layer ensures that the diverse information captured by the knowledge-guided block into the feature maps is effectively concatenated. After this process, we obtain a concatenated 2D feature

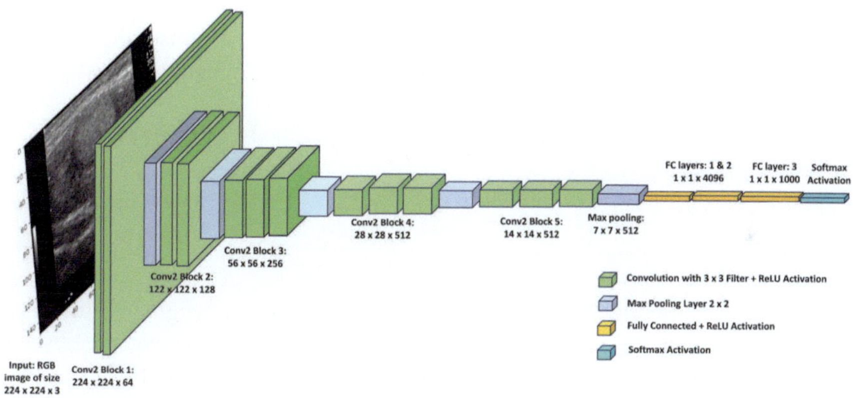

Fig. 5 The VGG-16 architecture

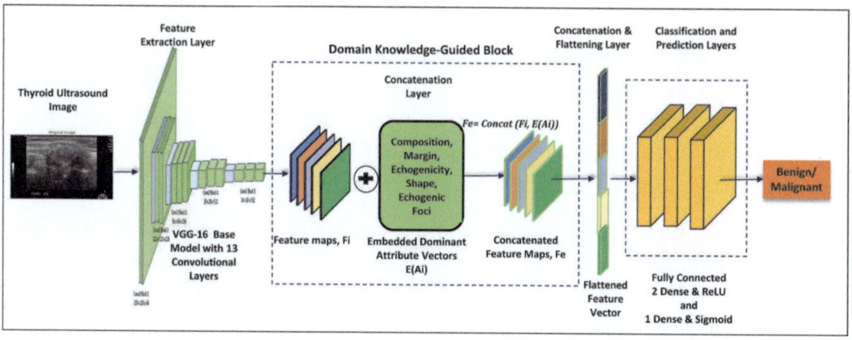

Fig. 6 A detailed overview of layers of our proposed deep learning architecture

map. To prepare this information for classification, the flattening layer transforms all the individual feature maps into a single, long, one-dimensional vector. This flattened vector, containing all the extracted features from the image, is then fed into fully connected layers of the neural network.

Classification and Prediction Layers. In the classification and prediction layers, 3 dense layers are used which are responsible for combining the high-level features learned by the convolutional layers and making final predictions. The first two dense layers perform intermediate processing on the concatenated features. The activation function used is Rectified Linear Unit (ReLU) activation to introduce non-linearity. The output generated by these layers is an intermediate feature representation that acts as a foundation for the final classification.

The final dense layer is responsible for the final classification of thyroid nodules. As activation function for binary classification (cancer vs. non-cancer), a sigmoid activation function is used. It produces the final prediction, representing the probability of the thyroid nodule being cancerous. These last three layers collectively form the decision-making part of the proposed network. The dense layers contribute to the extraction of high-level features and the final classification of thyroid nodules based on the learned representations.

Grad-CAM Heatmap Generation. The Grad-CAM technique utilises the gradients of the classification score, to identify the parts of an input image that most impact the classification score.

The weight of each feature map is computed as per the below given Eq. 1.

$$\alpha_C^k = \frac{1}{z} \sum_i \sum_j \frac{\partial y^C}{\partial A_{ij}^k} \tag{1}$$

The equation provided is used to compute the importance or weight (α_C^k) assigned to each feature map (A_{ij}^k) in the final layer of a neural network. This weight represents the contribution of the corresponding feature map to the prediction of a specific class c.

Y^C: The score or activation of class c in the final layer of the neural network. It represents the network's confidence in predicting class c.
A_{ij}^k: The activation of the k-th feature map at spatial position (i,j) in the final layer. This is the output of a convolutional layer.
(∂Y^c)/(∂ 〖A_(i, j)〗 ^k): The partial derivative of the predicted class score with respect to the activation of the k-th feature map at position (i, j).
∑i ∑j: Summation over all spatial positions in the feature map.
z: A normalization term to scale the importance weights.

The gradient of the predicted class score is calculated relative to the feature maps in the final convolutional layer. Gradients are aggregated spatially by applying global average pooling (GAP) across each feature map. Weighted sum of feature maps is computed using the computed gradients as weights.

ReLU activation is applied to the obtained weighted sum. The resulting heatmap is upsampled to the original input image size. The Grad-CAM heatmap highlights the regions of the input image that contribute the most to the final prediction for a particular class. Pixels with higher values in the heatmap correspond to regions that strongly influence the model's decision.

4 Results

Deep Learning models are trained to analyse large medical images, patient records, and other clinical datasets to identify patterns and make predictions. Our proposed knowledge-guided pre-trained model can analyse thyroid ultrasound images, to predict the likelihood of malignancy with high accuracy.

4.1 Experimental Environment

The experiments with VGG-16 and Inception-v3 models on image datasets are conducted on Google Colab Pro with V100/A100 Nvidia GPU, Python 3.10.11 and Keras 2.12.0 with TensorFlow 2.12.0.

Python libraries including pandas, numpy, sklearn, bs4, pillow, glob, and VGG-16 are used. The parameter and hyperparameters of the proposed architecture are summarised in Table 1.

Table 1 Parameters and hyperparameters of proposed deep learning architecture

Parameters/hyperparameters	Value
Activation function	ReLU
Final layer activation	Sigmoid
Loss function	Binary cross entropy
Dropout	30%
Epochs	200
Learning rate	$2 \times e^{-5}$
Batch size	20
Input image size	$150 \times 150 \times 3$
Trainable parameters	9,177,089
Optimizers	RMSProp

4.2 Ablation Studies

In the ablation study, certain elements are systematically disabled or modified to observe the effects on the system's behavior. The goal is to gain insights into the importance of different elements and understand their contributions to the system's performance. Primarily, the role of dataset pre-processing steps and the fine-tuning using pre-trained VGG-16 base model are monitored in ablation study.

Selection of Segmentation. The thyroid ultrasound image dataset is pre-processed with segmentation and subsequent augmentation. The nodule is segmented around the region of interest (ROI) and cropped around the annotated region. This dataset is used to train the deep learning model. Similarly, only augmentation techniques are applied to the dataset and the model is trained with this dataset.

Fine-Tuning Strategies for VGG-16 Conv2 Layers. This study investigates the impact of fine-tuning strategies on the performance of a VGG-16 baseline model for image classification. A block-wise ablation approach is employed, where layers in the convolutional blocks are gradually unfrozen and retrained. Initially, the convolutional blocks of the VGG-16 model are used as a baseline, and all 5 conv2 layers are frozen to preserve pre-trained features. A dense classifier is added on top of this model for classification and results are observed.

The proposed knowledge-guided block is added with a concatenation and flattening layer. The dense classifier is added and trained on top of these layers using the dataset. Again, the accuracy is monitored. The convolutional layers are then gradually unfreezed block by block and the model is trained. The classification accuracy is again observed. Unfreezing and fine-tuning Block 5's Conv2 layers exhibited substantial improvements in classification accuracy. With the integration of knowledge-guided block to the VGG-16 model, accuracy shows an upward trend. The results are summarised and shown in Table 2.

Table 2 Ablation study results

VGG-16 base model with dense layers			Proposed knowledge-guided model	
Dataset pre-processing	No segmentation	Segmentation	No segmentation	Segmentation
Frozen all blocks	*89.68*	*88.40*	*89.53*	*91.55*
Unfrozen Conv2 layers of 2nd block	*89.77*	*88.8*	*87.12*	*90.23*
Unfrozen Conv2 layers of 3rd block	*87.77*	*87.5*	*88.6*	*89.11*
Unfrozen Conv2 layers of 4th block	89.45	89.21	86.78	90.79
Unfrozen Conv2 layers of 5th block	**94.97**	90.78	91.12	92.84

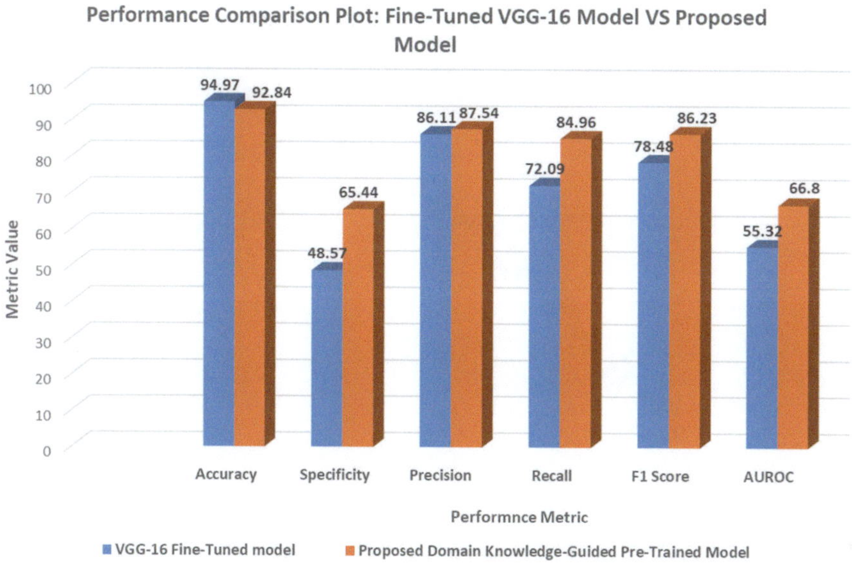

Fig. 7 Comparison plots: performance metrics of fine-tuned VGG-16 model and proposed model

The fine-tuned VGG-16 with fully connected dense classification layers showed an excellent accuracy of 94.97%, while our proposed model with the fine-tuned VGG-16 layer showed an accuracy of 92.84%. Other performance metrics were also calculated, and our proposed model showed better performance than the fine-tuned VGG-16 model as shown in Fig. 7.

4.3 *Visualisations*

In this subsection, visual insights into our proposed model, leveraging tools such as convolutional layer visualisations and Grad-CAM heatmaps are presented. Grad-CAM heatmaps display regions in input images that contribute most significantly to classification decisions.

Figures 8 and 9 show the accuracy and loss function plots of our proposed model trained on images with the fine-tuning of VGG-16 blocks with the unfreezing of all 3 layers of block 5. Figures 10 and 11 show accuracy and loss function plots of segmented image datasets trained with our proposed model with and without fine-tuning using the VGG-16 base block 5 convolutional layers. Figure 12 shows a malignant nodule and Grad-CAM heatmap visualisations with highlighted portion of the nodule which is used in the prediction process.

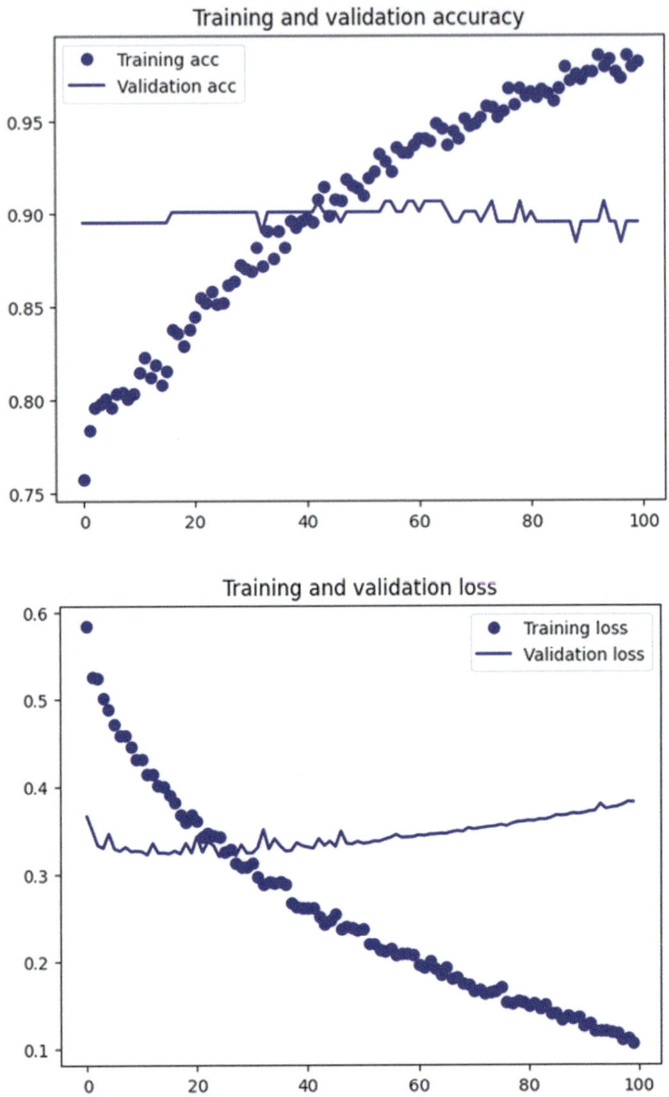

Fig. 8 Accuracy and loss function plots of image dataset trained with the proposed model with frozen convolutional layers of VGG-16

5 Discussions and Limitations

The proposed model displays good accuracy and the insights gained from ablation studies, and visualisations advance our understanding of the thyroid malignancy prediction task. The novelty of our method lies in the incorporation of domain knowledge into the deep learning architecture.

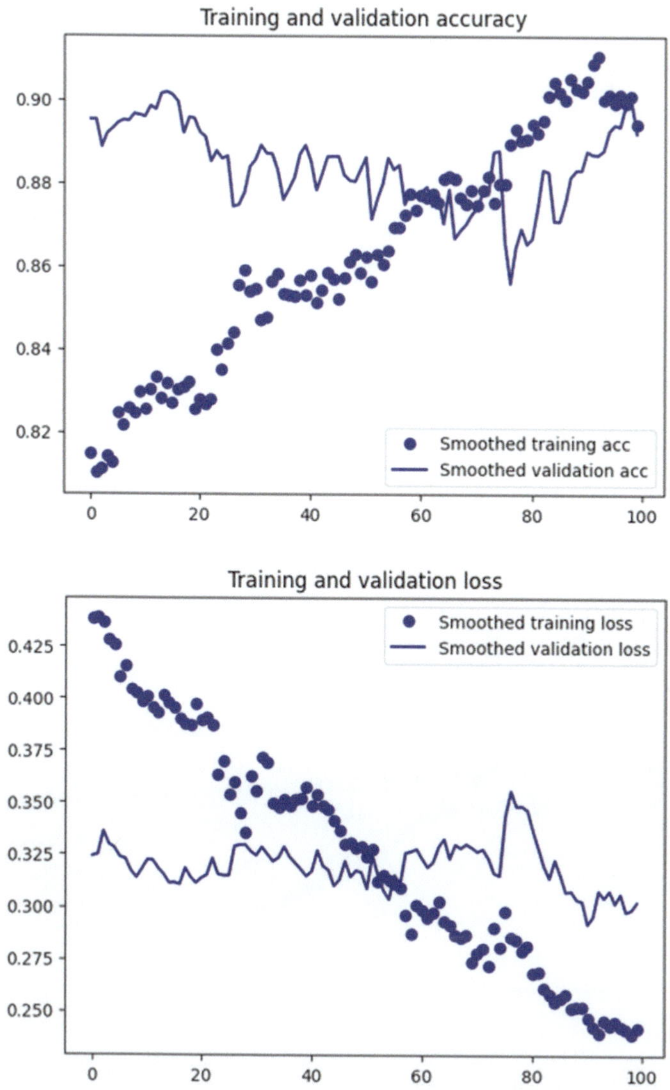

Fig. 9 Training and validation accuracy and loss function plots of image dataset trained with the proposed model with VGG-16 Block 5 conv2 layers fine-tuning

5.1 Comparison with Previous Studies

In the context of thyroid malignancy prediction, a comprehensive understanding of prior studies is important. Some key findings from relevant literature, highlighting methodologies and common trends are discussed here.

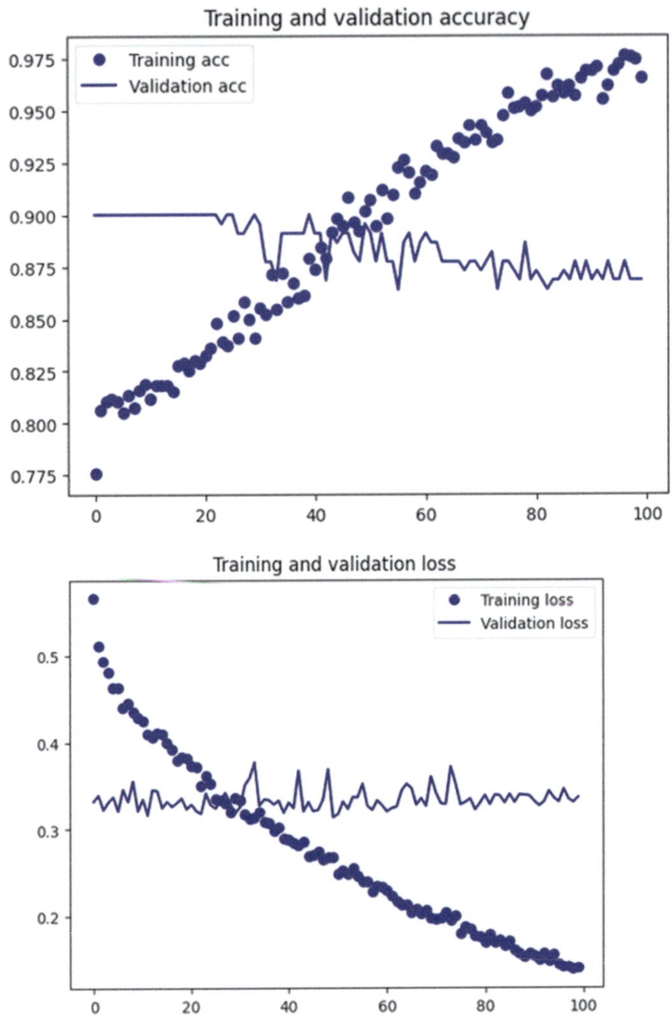

Fig. 10 Accuracy and loss function plots of segmented image dataset trained with proposed model with frozen VGG-16 convolutional layers

The authors of this paper conducted a study in 2024 [15], which introduces a new association-rule-based, attribute-embedded machine learning model that demonstrates improved classification accuracy. Additionally, it uses SHapley Additive exPlanations (SHAP) values as an effective approach for interpreting thyroid cancer diagnostic models. In the framework, association-rule-based analysis is used to identify frequently occurring attribute combinations within the dataset.

In a 2024 study [16], the authors of this paper proposed an advanced multimodal framework for thyroid cancer diagnosis, which combines ultrasound images with clinical data. The research is conducted in two phases: Phase I explores various

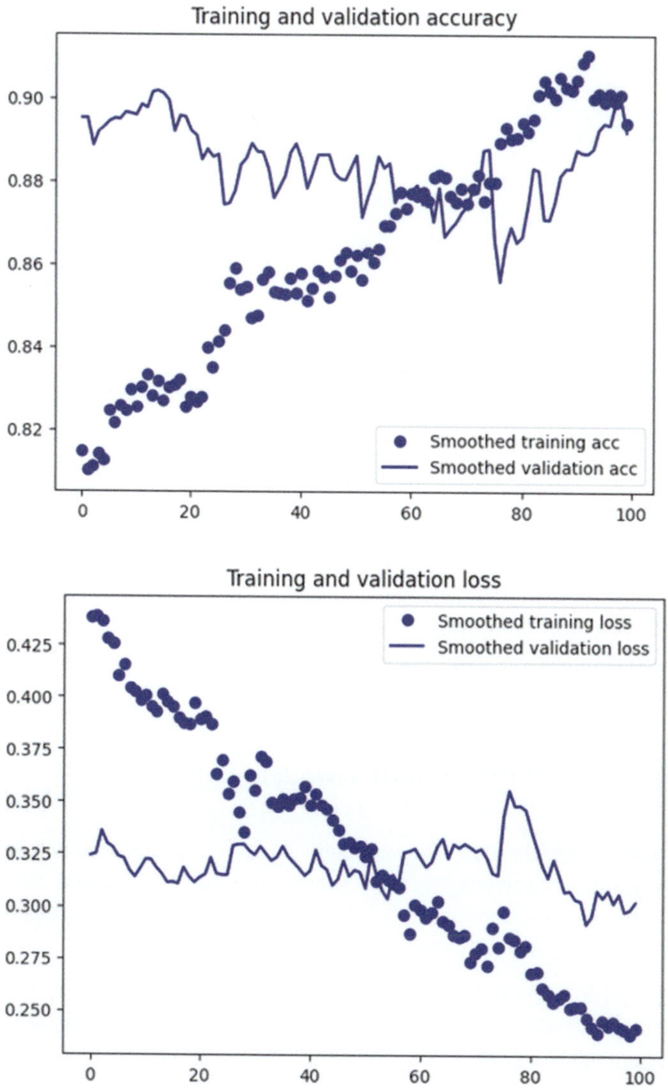

Fig. 11 Accuracy and loss function plots of segmented image dataset trained with the proposed model, with fine-tuned VGG-16 base model

machine learning and deep learning models to develop predictive models using ultrasound images and clinical data, selecting those with the highest accuracy for further evaluation. Phase II focuses on building ensemble models for multimodal prediction of thyroid nodules.

In 2021, a study conducted by Yi-Cheng Zhu and colleagues presented a thorough Deep Convolutional Neural Network (DCNN) framework that integrated transfer learning for the identification of thyroid cancer using ultrasonographic images [4].

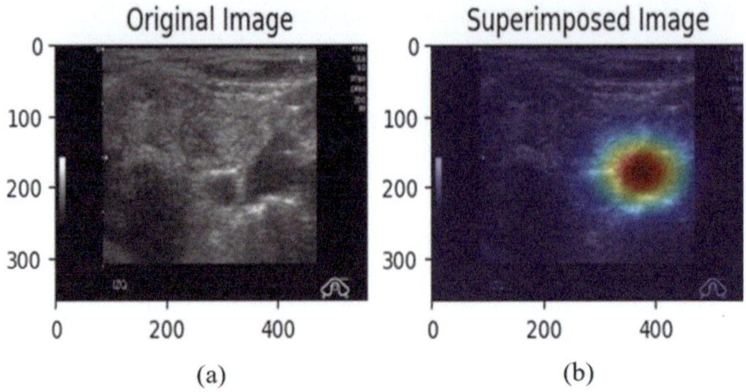

Fig. 12 Grad-CAM heatmap visualisations. **a** shows a malignant nodule and **b** shows the highlighted portion of the image with heatmap

Their methodology achieved an average classification accuracy of 86.5%. In 2021, Li and colleagues spearheaded a study [6] that introduced a classification network named CNN-F. This network, which integrates low-level and high-level features, was designed for the discrimination of benign and malignant nodules. The classification accuracy of CNN-F in the diagnosis of thyroid diseases achieved a notable 85.92%. Our proposed architecture achieved an accuracy of 92.84%.

5.2 Limitations of the Proposed Model

Computational Complexity. VGG-16 itself is a relatively deep model, and adding specialised kernels, knowledge-guided block, and fully connected dense layers significantly increase the computational complexity of the model. This makes training and inference computationally expensive and resource-intensive.

Overfitting. The introduction of a knowledge-guided block leads to overfitting, especially since the TDID dataset is not large or diverse enough. Regularisation techniques such as dropout are used to address this issue.

6 Conclusion and Future Direction

Machine learning and deep learning, two branches of artificial intelligence, offer vast potential in healthcare, driving innovations in areas like disease detection, treatment customisation, medical imaging analysis, and predictive modeling. The proposed model is a computational intelligent model of thyroid cancer diagnosis, trained on deep learning algorithms.

The proposed model is used successfully for the following tasks:

1. Nodule Classification: Distinguishing between benign and malignant thyroid nodules based on ultrasound images with good accuracy values of 92.84% comparable with current state-of-the-art methods.
2. Risk Stratification: Identifying patients with a higher risk of developing aggressive cancer, which facilitates early intervention, and ultimately improving the prognosis
3. Explainability: The thyroid prediction model is enhanced with interpretability through the application of Grad-CAM, providing valuable insights into the regions of interest and contributing to the transparency of the model's decision-making process.

In this research, we present a model designed for the transparent classification of malignancy in thyroid nodules. Grad-CAM heatmaps are used to visualise crucial areas in images influencing attribute predictions. The primary objective of our study is to ensure that domain knowledge-based deep learning contributes to medical imaging with results that can be easily interpreted. While traditional deep learning models excel at pattern recognition from vast amounts of data, they often lack an understanding of the specific domain they are applied to. In contrast, our model incorporates domain-specific characteristics from thyroid ultrasound images. Moving forward, our plans involve exploring multiple explainability techniques for more accurate heatmaps and refining the attribute prediction pipeline. Additionally, we aim to incorporate diverse datasets for improved outcomes.

Declarations Acknowledgements The authors would like to express their appreciation for the assistance and support provided by Dr. P. Rajan and Dr. Shahid Shameem from Aster MIMS, Kozhikode, Kerala. They are also grateful to Dr. Sandhya Susan Varghese, consultant physician; Dr. Indu Elizabeth Mathew, endocrinologist; and Dr. Bijoy Jacob Thomas, radiologist at EMC, Ernakulam District, Kerala, for their expert consultation on this research paper. Additionally, the authors wish to recognize the support from the Department of Research at Hindustan University, Chennai, TN, India, in conducting this study.

Funding The authors did not receive any funding for this work.

Conflict of Interest The authors declare no conflicts of interest regarding the current study.

Availability of Data and Materials The data supporting the findings of this study are publicly accessible and can be found at www.cimalab.unal.edu.co.

References

1. American Cancer Society (2023) Cancer Statistics Center [Online]. Available: https://cancerstatisticscenter.cancer.org. Accessed on 20 Oct 2023
2. Simonyan K, Zisserman A (2014) Very deep convolutional networks for large-scale image recognition. arXiv preprint arXiv:1409.1556

3. Selvaraju RR, Cogswell M, Das A, Vedantam R, Parikh D, Batra D (2017) Grad-cam: visual explanations from deep networks via gradient-based localization. In: Proceedings of the IEEE international conference on computer vision, pp 618–626
4. Zhu Y-C, AlZoubi A, Jassim S, Jiang Q, Zhang Y, Wang Y-B, Ye X-D, Du H (2021) A generic deep learning framework to classify thyroid and breast lesions in ultrasound images. Ultrasonics 110:106300. ISSN: 0041-624X. https://doi.org/10.1016/j.ultras.2020.106300
5. Warrier GS, Amirthalakshmi TM, Nimala K, Thaj Mary Delsy T, Stella Rose Malar P, Ramkumar G, Raju R, Teekaraman Y (2022) Automated recognition of cancer tissues through deep learning framework from the photoacoustic specimen. Hindawi, vol 2022. Article ID: 4356744. https://doi.org/10.1155/2022/4356744
6. Li W, Cheng S, Qian K, Yue K, Liu H (2021) Automatic recognition and classification system of thyroid nodules in CT images based on CNN. Comput Intell Neurosci 2021:5540186. PMID: 34135949; PMCID: PMC8175135. https://doi.org/10.1155/2021/5540186
7. Zhou B, Khosla A, Lapedriza A, Oliva A, Torralba A (2016) Learning deep features for discriminative localization. In: Proceedings of the IEEE conference on computer vision and pattern recognition. Las Vegas, NV, USA, 27–30 June 2016, pp 2921–2929
8. Cogswell M, Das A, Vedantam R, Parikh D, Batra D (2017) Grad-cam: visual explanations from deep networks via gradient-based localization. In: Proceedings of the IEEE International conference on computer vision. Venice, Italy, 22–29 October 2017, pp 618–662
9. Zhao H, Zheng C, Zhang H, Rao M, Li Y, Fang D, Huang J, Zhang W, Yuan G (2023) Diagnosis of thyroid disease using deep convolutional neural network models applied to thyroid scintigraphy images: a multicenter study. Front Endocrinol 14. https://www.frontiersin.org/articles/10.3389/fendo.2023.1224191
10. Choudhury AR, Mihail RP, Chiriac SD (2023) Prediction of thyroid malignancy using contextual semantic interpretability from sonograms. In: Proceedings of the 16th International joint conference on biomedical engineering systems and technologies (BIOSTEC 2023)—volume 2: BIOIMAGING, pp 94–101. https://doi.org/10.5220/0011670900003414
11. Di Song, Jincao Yao, Yitao Jiang, Siyuan Shi, Chen Cui, Liping Wang, Lijing Wang, Huaiyu Wu, Hongtian Tian, Xiuqin Ye, Di Ou, Wei Li, Na Feng, Weiyun Pan, Mei Song, Jinfeng Xu, Dong Xu, Linghu Wu, Fajin Dong, A new xAI framework with feature explainability for tumors decision-making in Ultrasound data: comparing with Grad-CAM, Computer Methods and Programs in Biomedicine, Volume 235, 2023, 107527, ISSN 0169-2607, https://doi.org/10.1016/j.cmpb.2023.107527
12. Pedraza L, Vargas C, Narvaez F, Duran O, Munoz E, Romero E (2015) An open access thyroid ultrasound-image database. In: Proceedings of the 10th International symposium on medical information processing and analysis. Cartagena de Indias, Colombia, 28 January 2015, pp 1–6
13. Horvath E, Majlis S, Rossi R, Franco C, Niedmann JP, Castro A et al (2009) An ultrasonogram reporting system for thyroid nodules stratifying cancer risk for clinical management. J Clin Endocrinol Metab 94(5):1748–1751
14. Ahmad H, Van Der Lugt A. TI-RADS—Thyroid imaging reporting and data system [Online]. Available: https://radiologyassistant.nl/head-neck/ti-rads/ti-rads. Accessed Sep 2023
15. Sankar S, Sathyalakshmi S (2024) A study on the explainability of thyroid cancer prediction: SHAP values and association-rule based feature integration framework. Comput Mater Continua 79(2)
16. Sankar S, Sathyalakshmi S (2024) Thyroid cancer diagnosis with machine learning: a multimodal ensemble approach for clinical decision support. Int J Intell Syst Appl Eng (IJISAE) 12(2):523–535

Aroma Detection: A Brief Study on Olfactory Science Using AI

Muhammed Mizhab, K. S. Divya, Bovas Eldho, S. Nandana, and V. B. Gowri

Abstract The paper aims to explore the intricacies of scent identification, conducting comprehensive research to uncover the underlying mechanisms of various odors. The main focus is on investigating the development of an effective aroma detection system capable of distinguishing between different scents, at a smaller scale. By integrating disciplines like signal processing, Machine Learning, and olfactometry, the aim is to gather insights that hold relevance across diverse sectors, including but not limited to food, safety, and environmental monitoring. Through experimentation and analysis, this paper seeks to shed light on the significance of scent detection through a cost-effective method.

Keywords Olfactometry · Groves Multichannel v2 Sensor · Classification by odor

1 Introduction

When it comes to digitizing senses, technology has been able to emulate three senses, viz., touch, sight, and sound. Smell is where the current technology significantly lacks. The paper aims to bring forth a budget-friendly method to tackle this problem.

Existing smell identification systems are not only costly but are also often impractical for small-scale applications. Leveraging our understanding and utilization of olfactory information, the goal is to develop an artificial nose capable of identifying different smells and predicting the associated organic sample using a cost-effective and modular aroma detection system.

The current landscape of aroma detection systems is characterized by inherent challenges, particularly concerning accuracy and affordability. Additionally, existing systems often lack accessibility for small-scale applications. Addressing these limitations, the aim is to develop an aroma detection system that is not only cost-effective but also modular in design. The existing papers delving into the olfactory domain and it's current state have been discussed further in the following section.

M. Mizhab (✉) · K. S. Divya · B. Eldho · S. Nandana · V. B. Gowri
Muthoot Institute of Technology and Science, Varikoli, Puthencruz, India
e-mail: themizhabwork@gmail.com

G. K. Rajanikant and P. Pré (eds.), *Perspectives on Global Transformation*, Lecture Notes in Electrical Engineering 1368, https://doi.org/10.1007/978-981-96-6707-9_2

2 Background

Olfactory research has witnessed significant advancements leveraging various technologies. Deep learning, specifically applied to mass spectra, contributes to predicting chemical odor traits [1]. Another approach utilizes Principal Odor Map (POM), employing graph neural networks to predict odor quality with a correlation of 0.91 to human panelists [2]. Additionally, artificial olfaction benefits from nano-engineered materials in gas sensor arrays, providing advantages in high surface area and precise control for enhanced sensing mechanisms [3]. Electronic nose (e-nose) technology emerges as a solution for detecting food adulteration, offering swift and reliable identification through selective MOS gas sensors [4]. A novel approach focuses on using VOC sensors to detect Parkinson's disease, demonstrating a non-intrusive and cost-effective method [5].

In the realm of virtual reality, a handheld olfactory display attached to an HTC Vive VR controller enhances the sense of presence in VR environments, showing potential applications in gaming, education, and therapy [6]. Chemical sensors, inspired by biological processes, are proposed for mobile robots to track odor traces with improved desaturation time for real-time odor detection [7]. Bioinspired electronic olfactory systems, utilizing spike-based signal transmission, aim for portable and personalized applications in the Internet of Things (IoT) era [8].

Efforts to enhance odor detection systems include an e-nose for alcohol and LPG odors, integrating an array of sensors and artificial neural networks [9]. A leading study explores the use of EEG data and deep learning to predict the type of odor a person is smelling, paving the way for innovative smell-based applications [10]. Graph neural networks (GNNs) prove effective in predicting quantitative structure-odor relationships, offering valuable insights into the molecular space representation of odors [11]. An electronic nose technology utilizing UV-activated SnO_2 nanowires operates at room temperature with low power consumption, presenting a cost-effective solution for gas and smell detection [12].

Traditional chemical sensors, including metal oxide sensors and conducting polymer sensors, play a crucial role in multimedia applications due to their simplicity and cost-effectiveness [13]. The concept of digital smell, utilizing electric pulses to stimulate olfactory receptors, has the potential to revolutionize online experiences by adding a new sensory dimension [14]. An IoT-based Indoor Air Quality Monitoring System, integrating low-cost sensors and the Raspberry Pi4, facilitates real-time monitoring of indoor air quality parameters [15].

3 Proposed System

3.1 Problem Statement

Olfactory science is a faction of study seldom delved into, which is possibly an up and coming field. However, current methods either lack efficiency or are expensive, leading to inconsistencies and potential hazards. To address this, there is a need for a reliable and user-friendly system that can swiftly identify and classify various odors. Leveraging technologies like Machine Learning (ML) and sensor arrays, the aim is to develop an innovative aroma detection system capable of accurately analyzing scent profiles in real time. The primary aim is to develop a cost-effective and modular aroma detection system capable of accurately classifying a limited range of aromas.

3.2 Proposed Solution

The proposed system aims to identify a limited range of aromas accurately. By adding different classes through data acquisition, to identify citrus fruits, garlic, ginger, coffee, and tea. Through the use of various ML models, the system aims to extract the relationship between the close data points.

The sensors will capture and transmit real-time data on scent profiles to the system. Each sensor within the array will possess varying sensitivities to different kinds of gases, enabling coverage of different odor compounds. These devices will feed data continuously into the system, providing a diverse dataset for analysis. By collecting the input from this sensor array, the system will establish correlations between specific sensor readings and distinct aroma profiles, enhancing its capability to accurately identify different scents. Leveraging ML algorithms, the system interprets these sensor data patterns to accurately identify specific aromas. The user interacts through an interface that displays detected scents. The ML algorithms that can be used to achieve this system include LinearSVC and ANN.

4 Methodology

4.1 Sensor Module

The Grove Multichannel Gas Sensor v2 employs various sensing technologies to detect and measure the concentration of specific gases and is based on MEMS technology, in which a miniature machine that has both mechanical and electronic components works to capture the sensor variation. Each of the four gas measuring units within the sensor module utilizes a different approach to sense its respective gas, namely, NO_2(*GM-102B*), C_2H_5OH(*GM-302B*), ***VOC***(*GM-502B*), ***CO***(*GM-702B*) sensor arrays [16]. It is connected to a microcontroller like, Arduino Uno, to obtain serial data as discussed below.

4.2 Dataset Acquisition

The sensor is initially preheated for a few hours to prepare for sample acquisition. The object samples to be collected are taken in different containers (zip-lock bags), such that each result will not interfere with one another. The serial sensor data through Arduino is collected through *CoolTerm*, a software for communicating with serial devices via USB. The readings acquired from the sensor include data for organic samples, viz., garlic, ginger, orange, tea, and coffee, in addition to background data, to represent the null condition of the sensor. Simply put, the process involves collecting data to effectively train the ML Model for accurate classification. This may involve exposing the gas sensors to the aromas emitted by fresh samples, each taken in a span of multiple days. As the sensor tends to give multiple results with changes to the environmental conditions, the data is taken as such to be inclusive of these varying conditions.

4.3 Data Preprocessing

The preprocessing step plays a crucial role in refining raw data collected from gas sensors before it undergoes classification by the ML Model. As the data acquired are spread across a span of multiple days, these datasets are combined and labeled with each sample type manually after removing duplicate records.

The next step involved is normalization through MinMaxScaler, which involves scaling the features of the dataset to a common range. Normalization ensures that each feature is treated equally by the ML Model, preventing any undue influence from features with larger scales. Additionally, the preprocessing phase involves transforming the data into a format that is optimal for model training and classification. This include steps such as converting categorical variables into numerical representations through encoding.

4.4 Training the Model

Fully connected neural network is used to extract the pattern between the given feature set. During training, the model is exposed to labeled examples from the dataset, where each example corresponds to a specific odor category. The model analyzes the features of the input data and identifies patterns that distinguish one odor class from another. This process involves adjusting the internal parameters of the model to optimize its ability to make accurate predictions. The dataset is typically divided into two subsets: a training set and a validation set. The training set is used to teach the model, while the validation set is employed to assess the model's performance on data it has not seen during training, helping to prevent overfitting.

The parameters are fine-tuned to ensure the accuracy of odor identification. The model hyper-parameters, like learning rate, number of dense layers, input layer size, etc., are adjusted based on iterative testing to optimize the performance of the model.

4.5 Testing

In the testing phase, input is derived from various odor samples collected by the Grove Multichannel Gas Sensor during real-time monitoring. The trained model analyzes patterns in the digitized data during the testing phase. Through this process, the system successfully classifies the odors of the trained samples, demonstrating its capability to adapt and accurately identify different aromas based on the knowledge acquired during training. The testing phase ensures the robustness and reliability of the system. This is done for samples of each additional class, to verify the correctness of the collected data. The model is then validated using 20% of the data collected during the data acquisition phase and the hyper-parameters are fine tuned subsequently.

5 Experiments and Results

The data acquisition phase is filled with uncertainty regarding the values that will correspond to the changes in the environment on each day. This is one of the major disadvantages of the system, which the research tends to tackle through the addition of more data on an up-to-date basis. This will ensure that almost all possible data of any particular class is covered.

Given in Fig. 1 is the data plotted for each gas, namely, VOC, NO_2, C_2H_5OH, and CO, of Background and Garlic samples across a span of 3 days. This data can show how fluctuating the sensor data can be with changing environment. The coupling of a temperature–pressure sensor can mitigate this by introducing new features. Comparison with results of existing paper [17] has been provided with our results.

Table 1 shows the model metrics: accuracy, precision and F1-score. The bolded first column indicates the chosen model for classification, following the metric observation.

Figure 2 shows the plot of loss of the model after training with the combined data of multiple days. As seen in the figure, the reduction in the loss value shows the improvement in the model's performance as training proceeds. The lower loss value indicates that the predicted values are closer to the actual value.

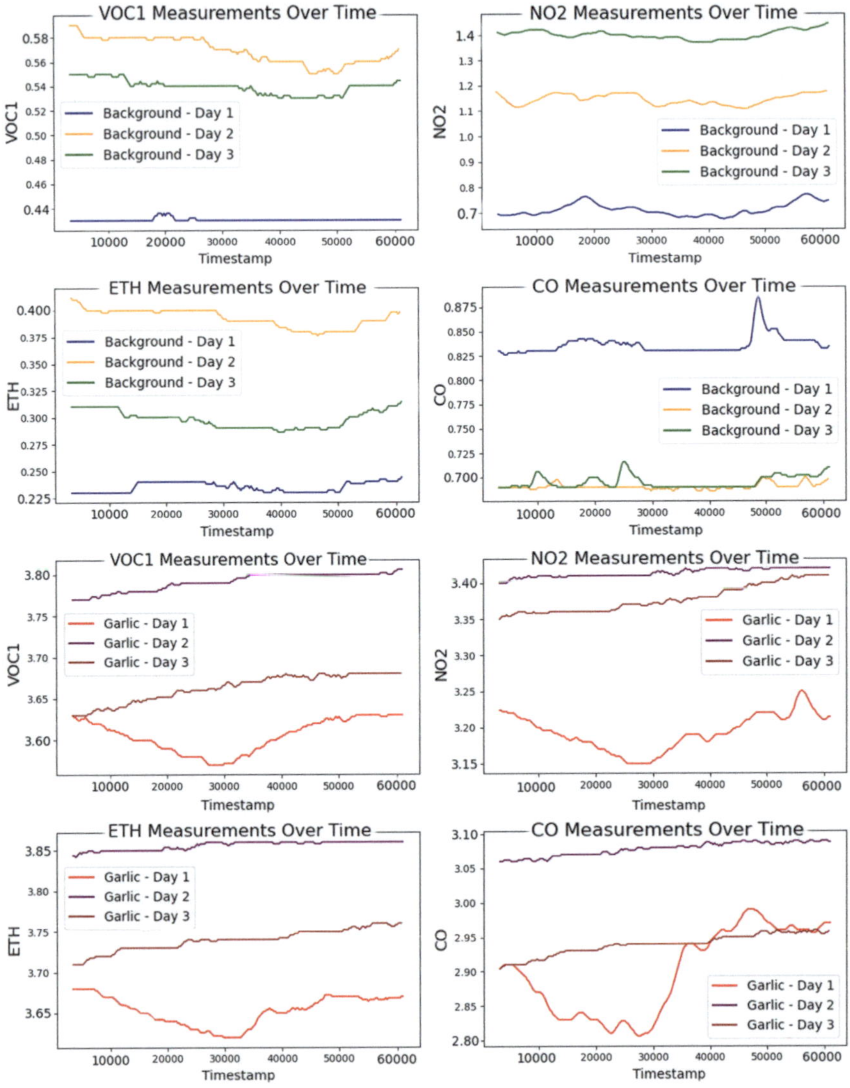

Fig. 1 Background and garlic data of separate gases over 3 days

Table 1 Model metrics comparison

	Accuracy	Precision	F1-score
ANN	**0.99**	**0.99**	**0.98**
CNN-LSTM fusion	0.96	0.93	0.93

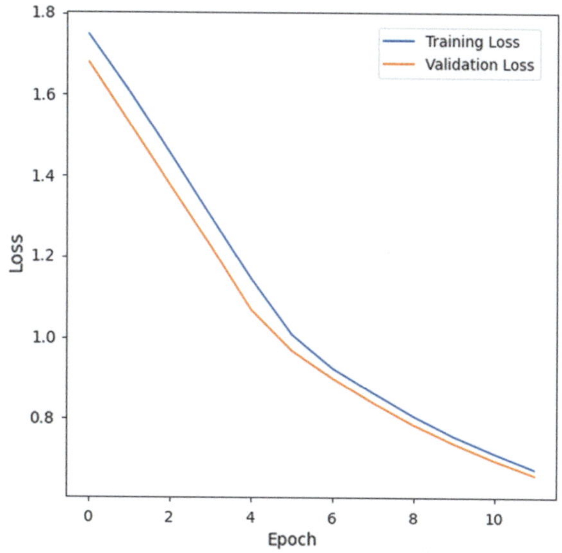

Fig. 2 Training and validation loss

Also, an observation during data acquisition was that the sensor was typically more sensitive to the Orange sample, and showed a correspondingly high value with respect to each sensor. However, the less sensitive data, including *tea* and *coffee* taken after, lacked accuracy until a certain cooldown period.

6 Conclusion and Future Scope

In summary, the aroma detection system represents a significant advancement in scent analysis technology, enabling real-time/cost-efficient classification. The system integrates an extensive dataset and classifies the odor sample in real-time. The methodology involves the systematic collection of sensor data, followed by digitization and the extraction of olfactory fingerprints through deep learning techniques. The integration of deep learning algorithms enabled the system to adapt and learn from feedback and improve its accuracy. Valuable insights were gained into the diverse applications in the fields, from food adulteration detection to early diagnosis of Parkinson's disease through smell signatures. Looking ahead, there are several promising scopes for further enhancement and expansion of the aroma detection system. Expanding the dataset and refining the training process for neural networks could enhance the system's accuracy and adaptability to diverse environments. Additionally, future applications could involve detecting rotten food and enhancing food safety measures.

Acknowledgements This research stands as a testament to the collective effort invested by numerous individuals and institutions who have played a pivotal role, both directly and indirectly. Heartful gratitude to Asst. Prof. Divya K S, for her relentless pursuit in this project being in fruition.

Further, we express our sincere gratitude to our mentor, Dr. Priya C V, for her invaluable guidance and motivation. Special thanks go to Dr. Sumam Mary Idicula, Head of the Department during our course period (2020-2024), for her critical assessment of our work and valuable suggestions. Also sincere thanks to Shawn Hymel, who has provided valuable insight regarding the functioning of the sensor, through his simplified artificial nose project.

References

1. Nozaki Y, Nakamoto T (2019) An olfactory sensor array for predicting chemical odor characteristics from mass spectra with deep learning. Methods Mol Biol 2027:29–47
2. Lee B, Mayhew E, Sanchez-Lengeling B, Wei J, Qian W, Little K, Andres M, Nguyen B, Moloy T, Yasonik J, Parker J, Gerkin R, Mainland J, Wiltschko A (2023) A principal odor map unifies diverse tasks in olfactory perception. Science 381:999–1006
3. Kim S et al (2021) Nanoengineering approaches toward artificial nose. Front Chem 9:629329
4. Roy M, Yadav BK (2022) Electronic nose for detection of food adulteration: a review. J Food Sci Technol 1–13
5. Kulkarni S et al (2020) Detection of Parkinson's disease through smell signatures. In: International conference on communication and signal processing (ICCSP)
6. Niedenthal S et al (2019) A handheld olfactory display for smell-enabled VR games. In: IEEE International symposium on olfaction and electronic nose (ISOEN)
7. Villarreal BL, Gordillo JL (2015) Bioinspired smell sensor: nostril model and design. IEEE/ASME Trans Mechatron 21:912–921
8. Han J-K, Kang M, Jeong J, Cho I, Yu J-M, Yoon K-J, Park I, Choi Y-K (2022) Artificial olfactory neuron for an in-sensor neuromorphic nose. Adv Sci 9:2106017
9. Nasir AM, Paul S, Mitra A, Prasad M, Banerjee PK (2016) On some aspects of odour detection system. Indian J Sci Technol 9
10. Benazzouz Y, Boudour R (2019) Integration of smell into the digital world. In: Third International conference on intelligent computing in data sciences (ICDS), pp 1–6
11. Sanchez-Lengeling B, Wei JN, Lee BK, Gerkin RC, Aspuru-Guzik A, Wiltschko AB (2019) Machine learning for scent: learning generalizable perceptual representations of small molecules. arXiv preprint arXiv:1910.10685
12. Adib M, Sommer M (2016) UV excited SnO_2 nanowire-based printed e-nose: potential application as burning smell detector and explosive detector. IEEE Sens 1–3
13. Ajemba P, Castro R, Al Istihad M, Mandal M (2003) A low-cost smell detection system for multimedia applications. In: IEEE International conference on consumer electronics (ICCE), pp 362–363
14. Karunanayaka K, Cheok AD, Vedadi S (2023) Digital smell: toward electrically reproducing artificial smell sensations. IEEE Access 11:50659–50670
15. Faiazuddin S, Lakshmaiah MV, Alam K, Ravikiran M (2020) IoT-based indoor air quality monitoring system using Raspberry Pi4
16. Grove Multichannel Gas Sensor V2. https://wiki.seeedstudio.com/Grove-Multichannel-Gas-Sensor-V2/
17. Narkhede P, Walambe R, Mandaokar S, Chandel P, Kotecha K, Ghinea G (2021) Gas detection and identification using multimodal artificial intelligence based sensor fusion. Appl Syst Innov

Single Channel EEG Classification for Motor Task

Joel George, Joel Jose, Lakshmi S. Nair, Sandra Skaria, P. Suresh, and Y. Sheena

Abstract The research presented explores the efficacy of a hybrid hardware/software architecture using a single-channel EEG for data acquisition and subsequent processing to achieve maximum accuracy in motor task classification for a Brain Computer Interface (BCI) System. The work focuses on classifying motor task-related EEG data using a single-electrode system and leveraging Machine Learning (ML) algorithms, in tandem with advanced filtering and feature extraction techniques. Results show that precise classification of motor tasks is possible using this hybrid Hardware–Software approach. SVM, Naive Bayes and Random Forest algorithms were used for the classification task and their efficacy was compared. An accuracy of 89% was achieved by the best classification model on data acquired using a single-channel EEG system.

Keywords BCI · Electroencephalography · Machine learning · Brain motor task

1 Introduction

Electroencephalography (EEG) is a non-invasive technique for monitoring the brain's electrical activity by placing electrodes on the external surface of the scalp. The recorded voltage variations are a result of ionic currents within the neurons of the brain. These EEG signals, commonly known as brainwaves, represent the neural oscillations generated through intercommunication among neurons. The method involves positioning electrodes on the scalp to collect EEG data, followed by a signal amplification stage, where the inherently weak EEG signal voltages are amplified. These amplified signals are passed through subsequent digital conversion stages before being finally stored in digital form.

Traditionally, multi-channel EEG setups are used for motor task classification. The placement of electrodes at the correct location is very critical for acquiring a strong and relevant signal. An increased number of electrodes increases the probability of

J. George · J. Jose · L. S. Nair (✉) · S. Skaria · P. Suresh · Y. Sheena
Muthoot Institute of Technology and Science, Varikoli, Kerala, India
e-mail: lakshmisnair1202@gmail.com

G. K. Rajanikant and P. Pré (eds.), *Perspectives on Global Transformation*, Lecture Notes in Electrical Engineering 1368, https://doi.org/10.1007/978-981-96-6707-9_3

their placement error which in turn adversely affects the system result. Our research aims to demonstrate the feasibility and efficacy of achieving precise classifications with just a single electrode. Motor tasks, such as movement intentions or actions, often elicit distinct EEG patterns, and our study delves into harnessing these patterns with a streamlined single-channel EEG approach. EEG signals are divided into five bands: delta (δ) (1–4 Hz), theta (θ) (4–7 Hz), alpha (α) (8–13 Hz), beta (β) (13–30 Hz), and gamma (γ) (>30 Hz) [1].

By developing a feasible EEG signal classification system using motor tasks, control systems can be developed for assistive devices such as motorized wheelchairs and prosthetics, that enable persons with disabilities to improve their quality of life.

2 Related Works

Prapas et al. [2] developed a BCI game that utilizes left–right motor imagery to control the game. It employed a two-step process for the development and evaluation of the BCI game viz Offline and Online Processing. In Offline Processing the raw EEG signals were acquired using the Neurosky Mindwave mobile headset and the OpenViBE platform was used to process the EEG data and extract relevant features. A Multilayer Perceptron (MLP) with two layers was employed for classification and the classifier was trained using a 10-fold cross-validation approach. In Online Processing the Muse 2 headband was used to capture real-time EEG signals. The Acquisition client in OpenViBE was used to receive the data from the headband. The real-time EEG signals were processed using the same methods as in the offline processing phase. The features were extracted and the trained MLP classifier was used to classify the mental commands. The classified instances were sent through a Lab Streaming Layer (LSL) stream to be used in the BCI game. The mental commands were translated into in-game movements of the avatar based on the classifier's output.

Zgallai et al. [3] proposed a prototype smart wheelchair that utilizes deep learning to assist blind and paralyzed individuals. The wheelchair is equipped with the Emotiv EPOC+ headset, Arduino Mega microcontroller, Raspberry Pi 3B+, ultrasonic sensors, Lidar Lite v3, and a servo motor. It is controlled by analyzing the EEG signals recorded using the Emotiv EPOC+. The recorded data is then transferred to a Raspberry Pi computer. The EEG data was processed using a convolutional neural network (CNN) consisting of three convolutional layers, three maxpool layers, and two dense layers. It takes the live EEG data and processes it in 2-s intervals. The output layer uses a softmax activation function with four nodes, corresponding to the four potential wheelchair states: forward, left, right, and stop. If the decision is to stop, the wheelchair enters a stop state. If the decision is to move in a specific direction, the corresponding command is sent to the L298N motor driver, which controls the movement of the wheelchair. Data from 10 volunteers were collected and analyzed to evaluate the performance of the deep learning algorithm. The results indicated that the CNN achieved a 70% success rate when using raw EEG data and a

96% success rate when using the Fourier transform of the data, focusing on specific frequency bands associated with brain waves.

Siribunyaphat and Punsawad [4] introduced a “QR code visual stimulus pattern” for SSVEP-based BCI as a visual stimulus presented to the user to elicit SSVEP responses. Four different flicker frequencies were used in the QR code pattern (5, 6, 7, and 8 Hz) each associated with a specific command for wheelchair control. The EEG signals were acquired using the Emotiv EPOC Flex EEG neuroheadset. The occipital area, specifically channels O1 and O2, was the focus for SSVEP signal acquisition. Two methods were used for SSVEP feature extraction: absolute power spectral density (PSD) and relative PSD. The QR code pattern was compared with a conventional checkerboard pattern to evaluate its efficiency. The results showed that the QR code pattern achieved higher accuracy and performance compared to the checkerboard pattern.

Gorjup et al. [5] explored signal processing and classification techniques for EEG-based BCIs that use motor imagery. They experimented with different filtering, feature extraction, and classification methods. Of the three datasets used, two were collected in noisy environments. The authors discovered that infinite impulse response (IIR) filters, known for their faster processing, were more suitable for signal processing tasks. Among the four feature extraction methods tested, band power features, which calculate the temporal power of a specific frequency band, proved to be the most effective. Butterworth IIR filters were used to extract band power features in three frequency bands: 8–12 Hz, 12–16 Hz, and 16–28 Hz. Two classification methods, linear discriminant analysis (LDA) and recurrent neural networks (RNNs), were evaluated. The results indicated that the linear classifier using LDA, combined with band power features, achieved comparable prediction accuracy to the RNN-based classifier but with greater robustness and computational efficiency.

Schirrmeister et al. [6] studied the ability of convolutional neural networks (ConvNets) to extract movement-related information from raw EEG data. They tested various ConvNet architectures, including shallow, deep, hybrid, and residual networks. The performance of these models was compared to a traditional method, filter bank common spatial patterns (FBCSP). Different design choices were investigated like batch normalization, dropout, tied loss, and splitting the first layer to improve accuracy. It was found that batch normalization and dropout significantly enhanced performance, with batch normalization being particularly beneficial for shallow networks and dropout for deep networks. The shallow ConvNets performed as well as the deeper ones, while hybrid and residual architectures were less effective. Overall, the deep ConvNets achieved decoding results comparable to or surpassing FBCSP.

3 Methodology

Experiments were designed for acquiring signals from healthy human subjects. The signals were collected using both dry and wet electrodes attached to the scalp of the human subjects. Equipment procured from Upside Down Labs' were used for signal acquisition and pre-processing. The different products used are as follows, Brain BioAmp Band (EEG stretchable band), BioAmp EXG Pill (circuit for signal amplification) and BioAmp Cable (cables to connect electrodes/EEG Band to the BioAmp pill). Figure 1 shows the different modules and their connection for intent classification used in this work.

3.1 Signal Acquisition

Subject performs the motor tasks eye blink, eye movement to left, eye movement to right and jaw clench with intervals of rest in between consecutive tasks. A three-electrode single channel system was used for capturing EEG signals from positions Fp_1, Fp_2 and A points according to the International 10–20 EEG electrode placement [7].

These signals were amplified by the BioAmp EXG pill which was then transmitted to a microprocessor board (an Arduino Uno development board) for recording and storage of the signals. The motor task was recorded in 5 s windows with a sampling rate of 10 kHz. The data was collected over three sessions of thirty minutes for each of the tasks. The data was stored as a CSV file. Each session consists of one task and rest (Fig. 2).

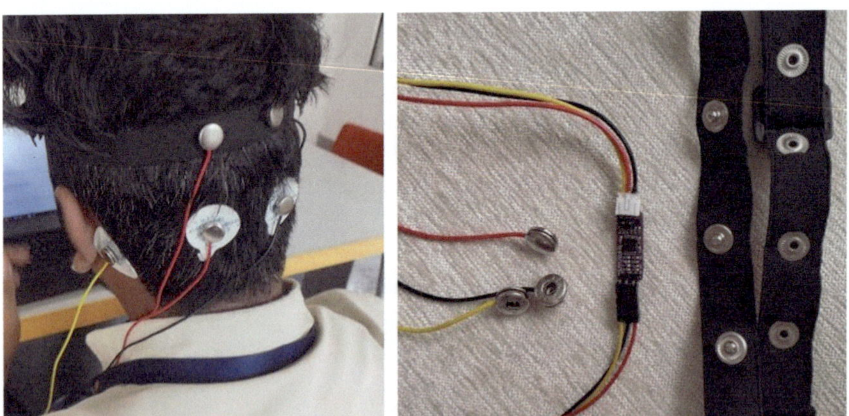

Fig. 1 Different modules and their connection for intent classification

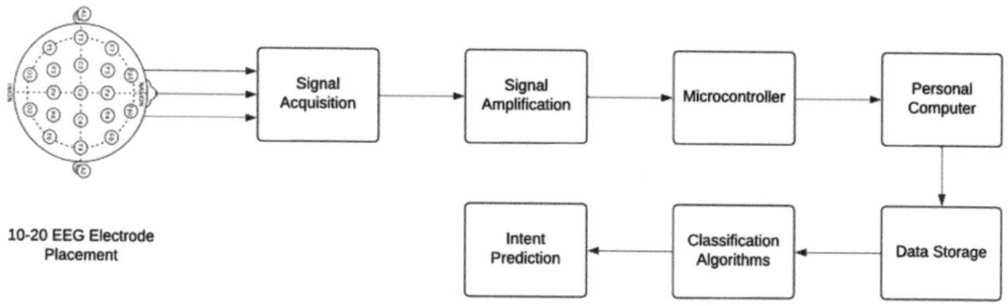

Fig. 2 System architecture: modules for EEG signal capture, recording and intent prediction

3.2 *Pre-processing and Dataset Creation*

The EEG signals need to be pre-processed to remove noise. A Bandpass filter of 1–19 Hz and a notch filter of 50 Hz is applied simultaneously while recording the signals for this purpose. The bandpass filter is selected to encapsulate the band of frequency in which the EEG signals of the required tasks are the most clearly capturable.

The CSV files containing readings for a single task (alternating between task and rest) were divided into chunks of 50,000 rows, labelled and combined into a single file. The chunks corresponding to the label 'rest' are removed and hence four files with readings corresponding to each task (eye blink, eye movement to left, eye movement to right and jaw clench) are obtained. For two class classifications, the files of left and right eye movement were combined to form the dataset while all four were combined to form a dataset for four class classifications.

For each chunk ten mathematical values were computed to act as inputs for the machine learning models, namely, mean value, variance, min value, max value, range value, median value, rms, total power, spectral entropy, zero crossings.

3.3 *Classification Algorithms*

Three classification algorithms (Random Forest, Naïve Bayes and Support Vector Machines) were studied and used to predict the intent of the subjects and the most effective one was selected. A brief description of the algorithms is presented below.

Random Forest: Random Forest ensemble learning models involve multiple decision trees, and Random Forest achieves this through two key mechanisms: bootstrap sampling and random feature selection. The algorithm creates multiple subsets of the dataset through bootstrap sampling and builds decision trees on these subsets. Randomness is introduced by considering only a subset of features at each split, promoting diversity among the individual trees. The model is trained by aggregating the predictions of each individual tree.

Naïve Bayes: It is a probabilistic classification method that uses Bayesian inference to calculate the probability of a class given the observed features; it estimates the prior probabilities of each class and the likelihoods of each feature given the class. The algorithm works under the assumption that features are conditionally independent, given the class label. This "naïve" assumption simplifies the computation of the posterior probabilities and is well suited for high-dimensional datasets.

Support Vector Machine (SVM): SVM operates by optimizing the hyperplane to achieve the widest possible margin between the classes in the feature space and identifying support vectors crucial for defining the decision boundary. SVM can be applied in both linear and non-linear scenarios. For linearly separable data, the SVM seeks a hyperplane that optimally separates classes. In cases of non-linear separability, kernel functions are used, such as radial basis function (RBF), to map the data into a higher-dimensional space where a linear separation becomes possible.

4 Experimental Results

The pre-processed data was used as input for various machine learning algorithms to categorize the motor tasks. The three algorithms were used to classify two class and four class classifications. For the two class classification eye movement to left and eye movement to right were considered and for the four class classification eye movement to left, to right, blink and jaw clench were considered (Fig. 3).

The metrics used are accuracy, precision and recall. Confusion matrices for all the algorithms were evaluated and are presented below (Figs. 4, 5, 6, 7, 8 and 9).

A confusion matrix determines the performance of a classifier system and in general, they are made up of four basic numbers.

Taking an example of a 2-class classification problem where two classes have to be identified namely Class I and Class II, these four numbers can be labelled as:

1. True Positive (TP): Represents the number of times a prediction of Class I agrees with an actual classification of Class I, it means that the system was able to generate a correct classification for Class I.

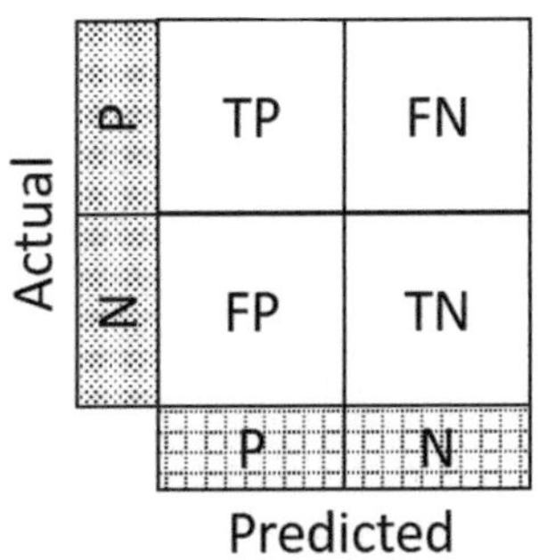

Fig. 3 Confusion matrix

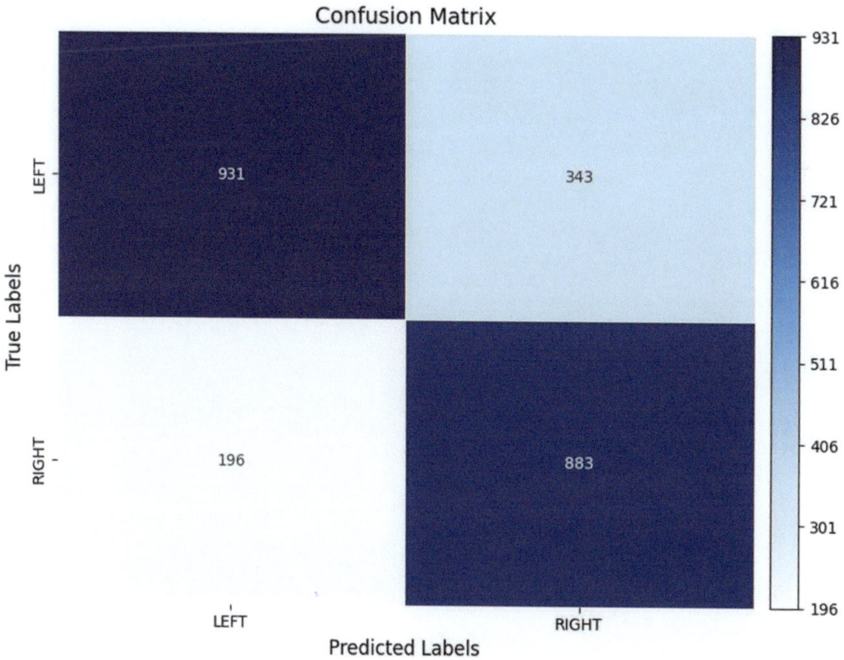

Fig. 4 Confusion matrix for Random Forest classifier for two class classification

2. True Negative (TN): Represents the number of times a prediction of Class II agrees with an actual classification of Class II, it means that the system was able to generate a correct classification for Class II.
3. False Positive (FP): Represents the number of times the class was predicted as Class I but was actually Class II. FP is also known as a Type I error.
4. False Negative (FN): Represents the number of times the class was predicted as Class II while being actually indicative of Class I. FN is also known as a Type II error.

The performance metrics of an algorithm are namely accuracy, precision, recall, and F1 score. These characteristics can be calculated using the TP, TN, FP, and FN described above.

The accuracy of the system/algorithm is represented as the ratio between the number of times the classes were classified correctly (TP + TN) and the total number of class instances (TP + TN + FP + FN).

$$accuracy = \frac{(TP + TN)}{(TP + TN + FP + FN)} \tag{1}$$

The precision of the system/algorithm to classify Class I is represented as the ratio between the number of instances where the predicted and actual class identification for Class I (TP) and the total number of class instances predicted as Class I (TP +

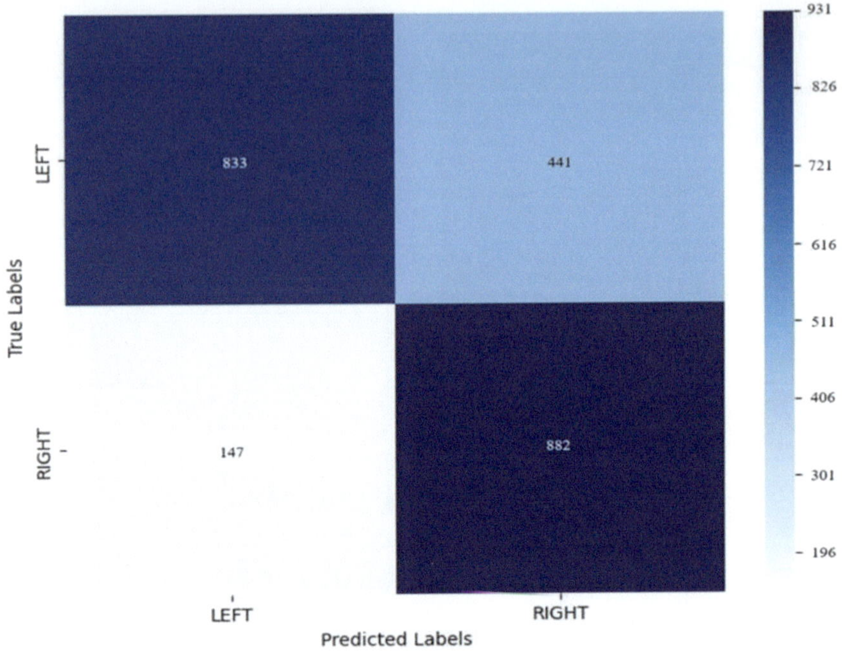

Fig. 5 Confusion matrix for Naïve Bayes classifier for two class classification

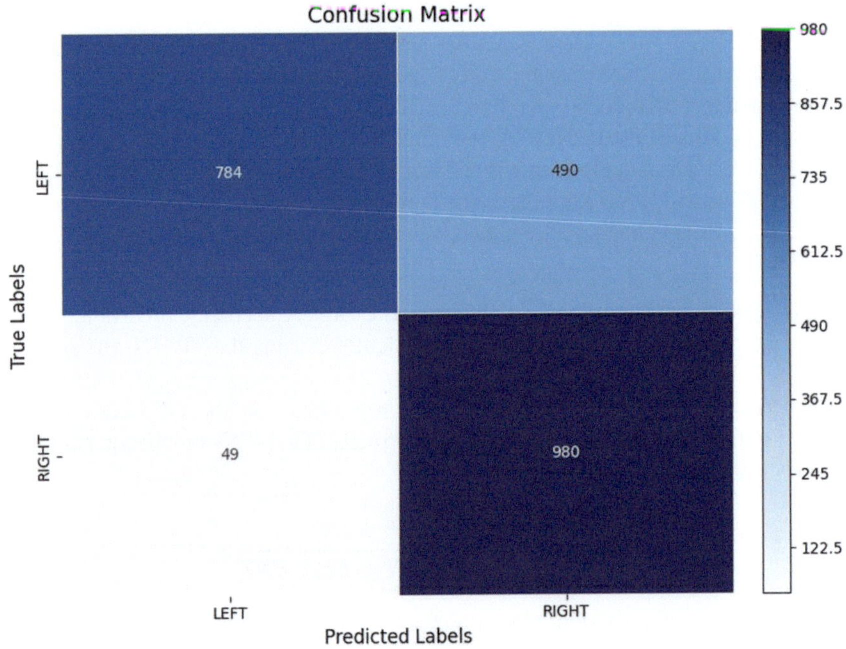

Fig. 6 Confusion matrix for Support Vector Machine classifier for two class classification

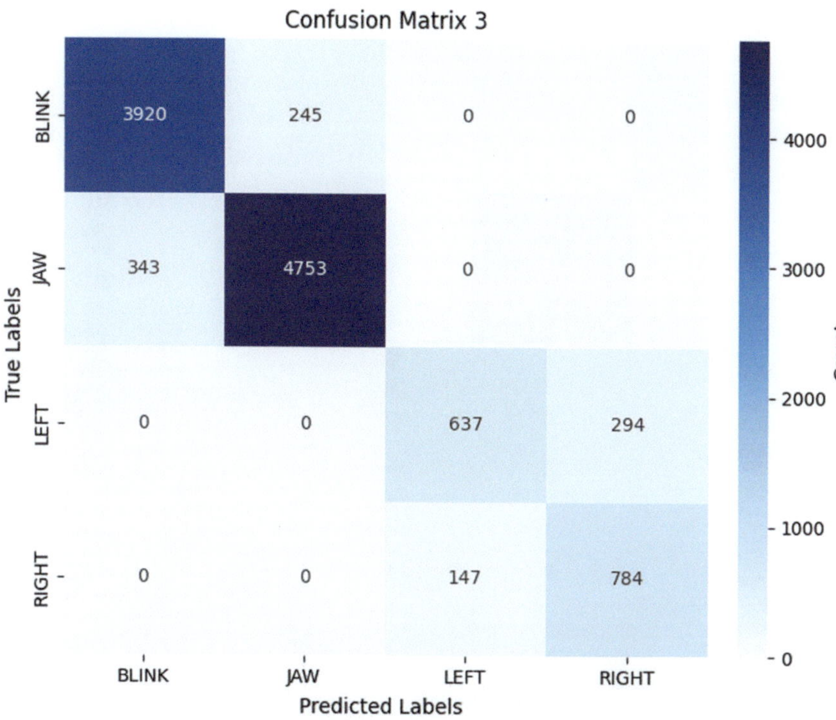

Fig. 7 Confusion matrix for Random Forest classifier for four class classification

FP).

$$precision(Class\,I) = \frac{(TP)}{(TP + FP)} \tag{2}$$

The precision of the system/algorithm to classify Class II is represented as the ratio between the number of instances where the predicted and actual class identification for Class II (TN) and the total number of class instances predicted as Class II (TN + FN).

The recall metric of the system/algorithm to classify Class I cases is defined as the ratio between the number of instances correctly identified as Class I (TP) and the total number of actual Class I instances (TP + FN).

$$recall(Class\,I) = \frac{(TP)}{(TP + FN)} \tag{3}$$

The "recall" metric is also sometimes referred to as the sensitivity of the system.

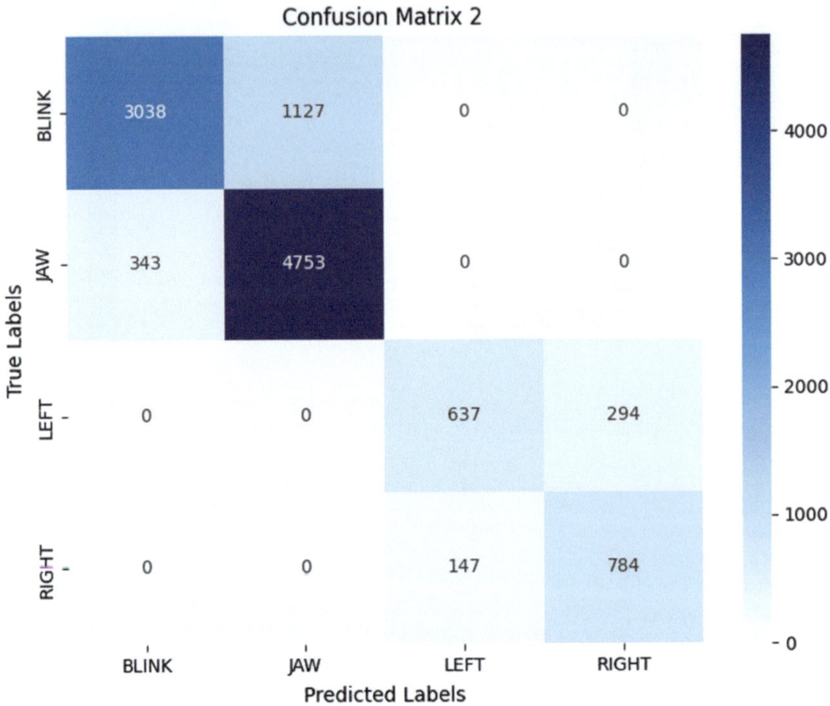

Fig. 8 Confusion matrix for Naïve Bayes classifier for four class classification

4.1 Comparison of Algorithms

Table 1 shows that the algorithm that gives the best result for two class classifications (left and rest) is the support vector machine.

Table 2 shows that for the four class classifications (left, right, blink and jaw) too SVM prevails as the better model.

From both of these, we conclude that the Support Vector Machine model gives the best classification. Hence for single channel EEG based brain signal capture and classification of motor tasks SVM is selected as the best algorithm with highest accuracy and precision.

4.2 Comparison with Existing Systems

Table 3 contains a brief comparison of some existing works with this system. As seen, this proposed system outputs a comparable accuracy of those with higher number of electrodes within economic constraints.

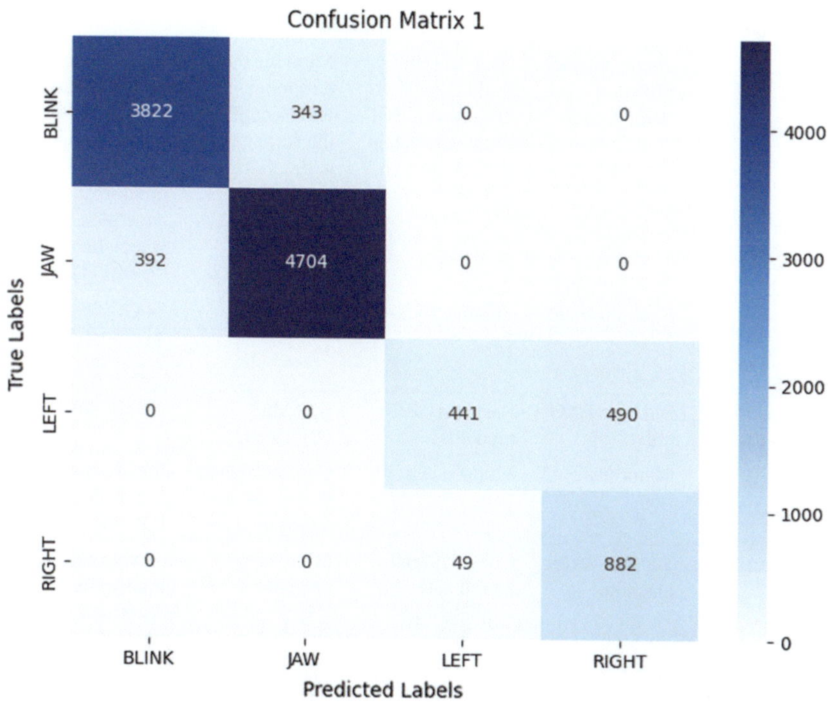

Fig. 9 Confusion matrix for Support Vector Machine classifier for four class classifications

Table 1 Comparison of evaluation metrics of different algorithms for two class classifications performed

Algorithms	Accuracy	Precision	Recall
Random Forest	0.77	0.77	0.77
Naïve Bayes	0.74	0.77	0.74
SVM	0.77	0.82	0.77

Table 2 Comparison of evaluation metrics of different algorithms for four class classification

Algorithms	Accuracy	Precision	Recall
Random Forest	0.89	0.89	0.89
Naïve Bayes	0.83	0.84	0.83
SVM	0.89	0.90	0.89

The method in this paper uses actual motor movement which is more tangible than abstract notion of imagery. It is a simple and easily implementable, yet effective method of classification. The use of only a single channel electrode enables the system to be highly cost effective with respect to its counterparts. This translates into cheaper production of end devices.

Table 3 Comparison of proposed system with existing works

Metrics	Single channel EEG classification	Deep learning AI application to an EEG driven BCI smart wheelchair [3]	Mind the move: developing a brain-computer interface game with left–right motor imagery [2]	Brain–computer interface based on steady-state visual evoked potential using quick-response code pattern for wheelchair control [4]
Headset	BioAmp Band	Emotive Epoc+	Muse 2	EPOC flex
Number of electrodes	1	14	4	32
Board/sensor/ analysis software	BioAmp EXG pill	Raspberry Pi 3 model B+	BlueMuse and OpenViBE	Cortex API
Nature of stimuli	Motor task	Motor imagery	Combination of motor task and motor imagery	Steady-State Visual Evoked Potential
Classification	Support vector machine	Convolutional neural network	Multi-layer perceptron	Absolute and relative power spectral density methods
Number of classes	Four	Four	Three	Four
Accuracy (%)	89	96	96.9	92
Overall cost	$43	$1035	$249	$1999

5 Conclusion and Future Scope

This paper presented a hybrid approach for the capture and analysis of brain signals using a single channel EEG Electrode. Single channel EEG electrodes with an SVM classifier have presented good accuracy, precision and recall in classifying motor tasks in individuals. The effectiveness of using deep neural networks for the classification of EEG data from single channel systems, particularly convolutional neural networks (CNNs) and recurrent neural networks (RNNs), holds promise in capturing complex temporal and spatial dependencies within EEG data. The effect of using multiple and/or hybrid algorithms needs to be studied more to establish the optimum number of electrodes for successfully meeting the system objectives (classification, categorisation etc.). The implementation of real-time processing for motor task classification can have significant applications, particularly in the development of brain-computer interfaces (BCIs) for neuroprosthetics or assistive devices such as wheelchairs.

References

1. Puthankattil Subha D et al (2010) EEG signal analysis: a survey. J Med Syst 34:195–212
2. Prapas G et al (2023) Mind the move: developing a brain-computer interface game with left-right motor imagery. Information 14(7):354
3. Zgallai W et al (2019) Deep learning AI application to an EEG driven BCI smart wheelchair. In: 2019 Advances in science and engineering technology international conferences (ASET). IEEE, pp 1–5
4. Siribunyaphat N, Punsawad Y (2023) Brain–computer interface based on steady state visual evoked potential using quick-response code pattern for wheelchair control. Sensors 23(4):2069
5. Gorjup G et al (2018) Development of a real-time motor-imagery-based EEG brain-machine interface. In: Neural information processing: 25th international conference, ICONIP 2018, Siem Reap, Cambodia, December 13–16, 2018, Proceedings, Part VII 25. Springer International Publishing
6. Schirrmeister RT et al (2017) Deep learning with convolutional neural networks for EEG decoding and visualization. Human Brain Mapping 38(11):5391–5420
7. Cobb W et al (1958) Report of the committee on methods of clinical examination in electroencephalography. Electroencephalogr Clin Neurophysiol 10(2):370–375
8. Teplan M (2002) Fundamentals of EEG measurement. Meas Sci Rev 2(2):1–11
9. Md Isa NE et al (2019) Motor imagery classification in brain computer interface (BCI) based on EEG signal by using machine learning technique. Bull Electr Eng Inf 8(1):269–275
10. Sita J, Nair GJ (2013) Feature extraction and classification of EEG signals for mapping motor area of the brain. In: 2013 International conference on control communication and computing (ICCC). IEEE
11. Al-Fahoum AS, Al-Fraihat AA (2014) Methods of EEG signal features extraction using linear analysis in frequency and time-frequency domains. ISRN Neurosci 2014

Agrobot: An Intelligent Crop Management Robot for Sustainable Crop Production and Precision Farming

K. Ankita Shenoy, Anu Yeldho, James Panikulam, Sagar S. Abraham, Angel Varghese, C. V. Priya, and Nivea Kesav

Abstract Agriculture is a vital pillar of a nation's economy. However, agriculture is both time-intensive and labour-demanding. Relying on traditional farming practices often results in significant losses for farmers, affecting both productivity and financial stability. Agrobot (Agricultural Robot) is the suggested solution to the aforementioned problems. The Agrobot is capable of carrying out multiple tasks such as planting, weeding, watering, and pesticide spraying, all made possible through robotics and automation. The robot is equipped with sensors and cameras that allow it to navigate through fields and identify crops, weeds, and other objects. The system is used to monitor and manage crops, identify problem areas, and predict potential yield. The Agrobot will also aid in minimising pesticide usage, which in turn helps to lower environmental pollution. Automation in agriculture is still in its nascent phase, and there are several challenges to overcome, such as developing algorithms that allow robots to perform complex tasks. But, advancements in Artificial Intelligence and Machine Learning are making these tasks increasingly attainable. With ongoing research and development, it is likely that Agrobot will become an increasingly important tool for agriculture in the future.

Keywords Agrobot · Navigation system · Crop and weed classification · Disease detection · Precision agriculture · CNN

1 Introduction

India, a nation with a population exceeding 1.2 billion, relies heavily on agriculture for sustenance. Over 70% of its citizens depend on agriculture for their livelihood, making it the backbone of the country's economy. The agricultural sector contributes approximately 16.1% to the nation's GDP and accounts for 10% of total exports. Over

K. Ankita Shenoy · A. Yeldho · J. Panikulam · S. S. Abraham (✉) · A. Varghese · C. V. Priya · N. Kesav
Department of Artificial Intelligence and Data Science, MITS, Ernakulam, India
e-mail: sagar.s.abraham@gmail.com

G. K. Rajanikant and P. Pré (eds.), *Perspectives on Global Transformation*, Lecture Notes in Electrical Engineering 1368, https://doi.org/10.1007/978-981-96-6707-9_4

60% of India's land is cultivable, making it the second-largest country in terms of arable land area [1].

Agriculture today remains a labour-intensive and time-consuming industry. Traditional farming methods often result in significant losses for farmers, both in terms of productivity and financial outcomes. This paper presents a new concept named Agrobot—an agricultural robot developed to perform tasks like seed planting and watering with enhanced precision and accuracy through the use of robotics and automation. By addressing issues of time constraints and labour shortages, this innovation aims to boost production efficiency and output [2]. In response to these challenges, the integration of robotics and artificial intelligence has given rise to Agrobots, autonomous systems designed to revolutionise agriculture. This paper introduces a cutting-edge Agrobot that amalgamates latest technologies to address key agricultural issues. The Agrobot incorporates a highly efficient irrigation system equipped with smart sensors for precise water management, alleviating water scarcity concerns. Complementing this, a sophisticated navigation system ensures the Agrobot's seamless coverage of vast agricultural fields, promoting optimal resource utilisation [3]. Furthermore, the Agrobot features an advanced classification model capable of distinguishing between crops and weeds, facilitating targeted interventions and minimising herbicide use. To enhance plant health monitoring, a robust disease detection model is integrated, enabling early identification of potential threats. This multifaceted Agrobot represents a significant leap towards precision agriculture, offering farmers a potent tool for sustainable, high-yield farming. The succeeding sections delve into the technical intricacies and real-world implications of each component, showcasing the potential of Agrobots to reshape the landscape of contemporary agriculture.

The structure of the paper is as follows: Sect. 2 covers related works, while Sect. 3 explains the proposed approach and methodology. In Sect. 4, the system components are outlined, followed by a discussion of the working principle in Sect. 5. Section 6 presents the experiments and results, with the conclusion provided in Sect. 7.

2 Related Works

LettuceBot is a robotic system created by Iron Ox that employs computer vision and machine learning to detect and eliminate weeds in lettuce fields. This robot utilises multiple sensors, such as cameras, LiDAR, and ultrasonic sensors, to construct a map of the field and pinpoint the location of weeds. It then uses a robotic arm to remove the weeds with a targeted laser.

DeepWeeds is an initiative by the University of California, Berkeley, utilising deep learning for weed detection in agricultural settings. The project has created a Convolutional Neural Network (CNN) capable of accurately identifying weeds, even in difficult situations, such as when they are small or hidden by other plants.

Plantix is a mobile app that uses machine learning to identify plant diseases. The app allows farmers to take pictures of their crops and upload them to the Plantix platform. The platform employs a deep learning model to diagnose the disease and offer treatment recommendations.

Monarch Tractor is an autonomous tractor equipped with various sensors and cameras that enable it to navigate fields and execute tasks like planting, weeding, and harvesting. The tractor uses machine learning to identify and track crops, as well as to avoid obstacles.

FarmOS is an open-source platform that allows farmers to collect and manage data from their farms. The platform can be used to collect data from a variety of sources, including sensors, cameras, and weather stations. FarmOS can then be used to analyse the data and provide insights to farmers that can help them improve their yields and efficiency.

3 Methodology

The functionality of the Agrobot is implemented in a systematic manner. The irrigation system uses intelligent sensors to measure soil moisture levels, allowing for accurate water delivery. The navigational system uses another set of sensors to navigate the field efficiently. The crop and weed classification and disease detection are utilised using cameras and machine learning algorithms trained on a variety of datasets, for precise and timely evaluations.

The revisions are discussed in the following sections.

3.1 Collecting Required Sensor Info and Data

Before the Agrobot was built, a thorough data collection process was conducted to inform the robot's design and functionality. This included deploying a network of high-tech sensors across the Agrobot's test sites to collect detailed environmental data. The sensors were strategically positioned to monitor key parameters, including soil moisture and temperature, to enhance understanding of the field's conditions. We also collected large image datasets using manual capture methods to focus on different crops and weed species. These image datasets served as the empirical base for machine learning models to analyse crops, classify weeds, and detect diseases. By thoroughly researching and cataloguing the details of the agricultural environment in advance, we made sure that the construction and subsequent operations would be informed by a strong dataset, making the Agrobot more effective in real world farming scenarios.

3.2 Training the ML Models

In order to develop the Agrobot, we trained two different machine learning models that are necessary for its autonomous operations:

Crop and Weed Classification Model: We created a diverse dataset of images of various crops as well as common weed species. We then trained the model to differentiate between crops and weeds to ensure accuracy during the robot's weeding tasks.

Disease Detection Model: We also carefully curated a dataset of crop images showing different disease symptoms. We trained the model to recognise subtle signs of diseases so that it could detect them early for proactive pest management.

3.3 Creation of the Agrobot

To optimise its performance, the Agrobot was created through a complex process of sensor integration and threshold parameter establishment. Every sensor that was placed thoughtfully on the robot was set to particular humidity, temperature, and soil moisture thresholds. Extensive research and field testing were used to define these thresholds in order to guarantee precise readings that corresponded to ideal agricultural conditions. The robot's ability to gather environmental data in real-time while operating was made possible by the integration of these sensors. Setting thresholds was essential for initiating particular actions, like watering in reaction to low soil moisture, in addition to sensor integration. Farmers will be able to make precise decisions for effective crop management and receive actionable insights thanks to the Agrobot's ability to autonomously adapt to changing field conditions thanks to the dynamic interaction between sensors and predefined thresholds [4]. Agrobots use a precisely engineered mechanism that uses a servo motor to accomplish seeding. The servo motor, which is safely mounted on the agrobot frame, is designed to regulate the release of seeds while taking depth and spacing into account. Reliable and effective autonomous seeding is ensured by integration with sensors and an efficient power supply.

3.4 CNN Model

The CNN (Convolutional Neural Network) architecture comprises various layers such as:

Convolutional Layer: A CNN is centred around the convolutional layer. It applies filters (also called kernels) to the input data in order to extract relevant features. Each filter slides across the input data, applying element-wise operations to generate a feature map that emphasises particular patterns or edges. The layer can have multiple filters to capture different features simultaneously.

Activation Layer: A non-linearity activation function is applied to each element in the output of the convolutional layer. Common activation functions, such as ReLU (Rectified Linear Unit), set negative values to zero while preserving positive values. These activation functions enable the network to learn complex patterns, making it more adaptable and capable of capturing intricate relationships.

Pooling Layer: Pooling layers are utilised to decrease the spatial dimensions of feature maps produced by the convolutional layer. Two prevalent types of pooling are max pooling, which identifies the highest value within a specified window, and average pooling, which calculates the mean value. The pooling process helps to downsample the data, enhancing the network's resilience to input variations and decreasing the parameter count, ultimately leading to better computational efficiency.

Fully Connected Layer: The data is flattened into a one-dimensional vector and fed into fully connected layers after undergoing numerous convolutional and pooling layers. In these levels, every neuron is connected to every other neuron in the layers above and below, emulating a conventional neural network. Fully connected layers facilitate high-level feature extraction and generate predictions based on the features that have been learned. They are often followed by an activation function and the output layer, depending on the specific task.

These are the key layers in a typical CNN model, but it's important to note that different architectures may include additional layers or variations of these layers to achieve specific goals. Understanding the flow of information through the convolutional, activation, pooling, and fully connected layers helps CNN models effectively extract and process features, ultimately making accurate predictions in various visual tasks.

3.5 YOLOv8 Architecture

The YOLOv8 (You Only Look Once Version 8) architecture comprises various layers that contribute to its object detection capabilities [5, 6]. Here's a brief explanation of each layer:

Backbone Network (Darknet-53): The backbone network is the feature extraction component of YOLOv8. In YOLOv8, Darknet-53 is commonly used as the backbone, and it consists of multiple layers of convolutional and residual blocks. This component of the architecture is tasked with extracting hierarchical features from the input image.

Neck Layer (PANet): YOLOv8 includes a neck layer, often implemented as PANet (Path Aggregation Network). The neck layer enhances feature representation by aggregating information from different levels of the feature hierarchy, aiding in object detection across various scales.

Detection Heads: YOLOv8 employs multiple detection heads, each responsible for predicting bounding boxes and class probabilities at different scales. These heads allow the model to handle objects of different sizes within the image effectively.

YOLO Head: The YOLO head is a critical part of the architecture, responsible for generating final predictions. It applies additional convolutional and fully connected layers to predict bounding box coordinates, objectness scores, and class probabilities. These components work together cohesively, allowing YOLOv8 to process input images rapidly while maintaining high accuracy in detecting and classifying objects. The architecture's flexibility and efficiency make it well-suited for real-time applications in computer vision and object detection tasks.

3.6 Testing

In order to guarantee the precision and dependability of the Agrobot's machine learning models in actual agricultural situations, a thorough and organised assessment procedure was employed during the testing phase. The models' capacity for classification was evaluated using a wide range of photos that depicted various crops, weeds, and possible illnesses. To replicate the dynamic nature of agricultural environments, the models were exposed to a range of environmental factors, lighting scenarios, and crop stages. The models' performance was thoroughly evaluated through the testing method, which integrated quantitative criteria like precision, recall, and F1 score. To improve the models' robustness and adaptability, incremental improvement was done in response to the testing results. The Agrobot's machine learning capabilities were put through a rigorous testing process to guarantee that they met high standards of accuracy. This set the stage for the robot's successful field deployment for tasks like precise crop management, disease detection, and weed identification.

4 Robotic System Components

The system architecture of a multipurpose agrobot shows how different components interact with each other using the TensorFlow YOLOv8 model (Fig. 1).

The system consists of the following components:

- User: The user interacts with the system through a Blynk UI, which can be accessed from a smartphone or tablet.
- Microcontroller: The microcontroller, Arduino Mega 2560 SAMD21 and ESP8266 controls the whole system. It receives commands from the app and controls the robot [7].

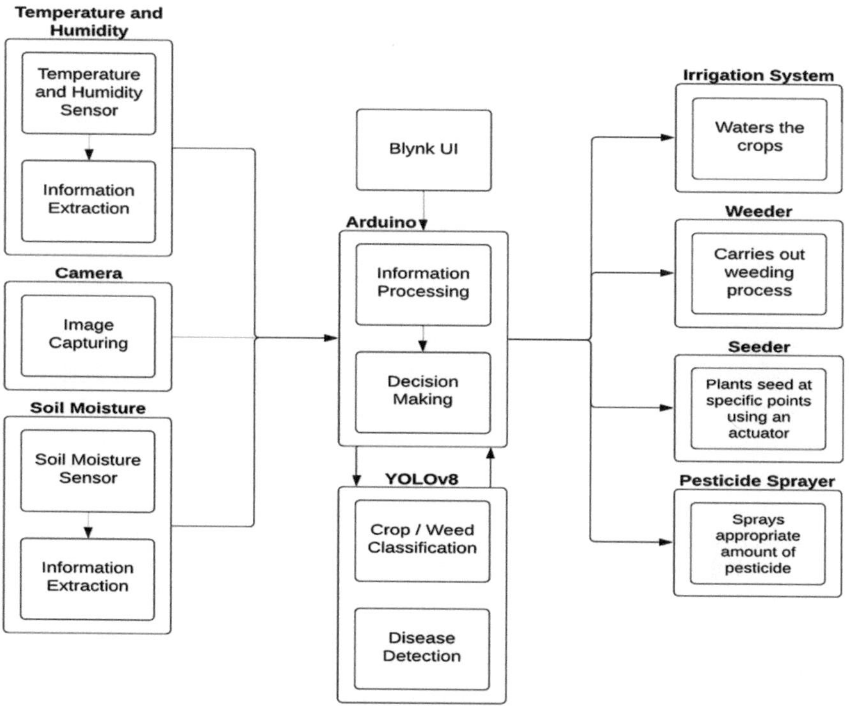

Fig. 1 System architecture

- Camera: The FPV camera captures images of the plants, which the YOLOv8 model utilises to detect and classify objects.
- YOLOv8 model: YOLOv8 is a state-of-the-art deep learning architecture designed for real-time object detection and classification.
- Actuators: The actuators are used to perform actions on the field, such as moving the robot, operating machinery, and applying pesticides.

The actuators include: Gear motors, Linear Actuators, water pump, regular motors, and servo motors.

5 Working Principle

The working of the system is as follows:

- The Blynk UI allows the user to communicate with the system by giving commands to the microcontroller. Blynk is a platform that lets users use an app to monitor and control devices.

- The Blynk UI issues commands to the microcontroller. These directives might include guidelines for carrying out particular farming operations, like weeding, pesticide application, or seed planting.
- The microcontroller interacts with the YOLOv8 (You Only Look Once, version 8) model by processing the commands that are received. YOLOv8 is a state-of-the-art algorithm for real-time object detection, enabling the recognition and classification of objects in visual data.
- The YOLOv8 model recognizes and categorises objects in the agricultural field by analysing camera images. This involves determining whether any plants, weeds, or other pertinent items are present.
- After it performs analysis, the YOLOv8 model returns the object detection and classification results to the microcontroller. The system receives feedback from this data regarding the condition of the agricultural field right now.
- When the microcontroller receives data from the YOLOv8 model, it triggers the relevant actuators. Devices that carry out physical actions are called actuators. In this case, they might be seed planting mechanisms, robotic arms for pulling weeds, or pesticide spray nozzles.
- In accordance with user commands and the outcomes of the YOLOv8 analysis, the actuators perform the intended actions on the agricultural field. For instance, the microcontroller might tell the weeding actuator to pull weeds if the YOLOv8 model identified a weedy area.
- Because of its modular and scalable design, the system is simple to modify to fit a variety of agricultural tasks. This implies that beyond the initial set of tasks, the system can be configured to carry out a variety of agricultural operations using additional or different types of actuators.

6 Experiment and Results

The application of YOLOv8 for crop-weed classification has demonstrated significant success in accurately distinguishing between crops and weeds within agricultural fields. Overall, the utilisation of YOLOv8 for crop-weed classification proves to be providing a reliable and rapid solution for optimising weed control practices and enhancing overall crop yield. The dataset comprises 1300 images featuring sesame crops alongside various types of weeds, each accompanied by image labels. Each image has a resolution of 512 × 512 pixels and is in colour. The labels for these images follow the YOLO format (Figs. 2 and 3).

To assess the effectiveness of the proposed algorithm, it's essential to consider specific metrics derived from the output, including True Positives (TP), False Positives (FP), False Negatives (FN), and True Negatives (TN).

$$\text{Accuracy} = (\text{TP} + \text{TN})/(\text{TP} + \text{TN} + \text{FP} + \text{FN})$$

Fig. 2 Crop-weed detection: weed detected

Considering 125 sample images, we assigned the following values for the variables.

$$TP = 48, FP = 1, FN = 3, TN = 37.$$

Table 1 shows that the average accuracy rate is 96%, reflecting the algorithm's strong performance. In comparison, the accuracy of the existing system ranges from 51 to 78% [8, 9]. The YOLO model is notable not only for its remarkable speed relative to other deep neural network architectures but also for its effectiveness in analysing both healthy crops and weeds [10, 11].

For plant disease detection, there are several existing systems that use models such as SVM, ANN, KNN etc [12, 13]. Conventional machine learning algorithms necessitate manual feature engineering and can struggle with high-dimensional and complex datasets [14, 15]. Traditional ML algorithms cannot differentiate between subtle differences in images (Figs. 4 and 5; Table 2).

Fig. 3 Crop-weed detection: crop detected

Table 1 Results of the predicted weed detection

	Proposed system	Existing system [4]	Existing system [8]
Data	Sesame crop and weed dataset	Sesame crop and weed dataset	Sesame crop and weed dataset
Method used	YOLO v8	ANN	Multispectral imaging
Accuracy (%)	96	51	78

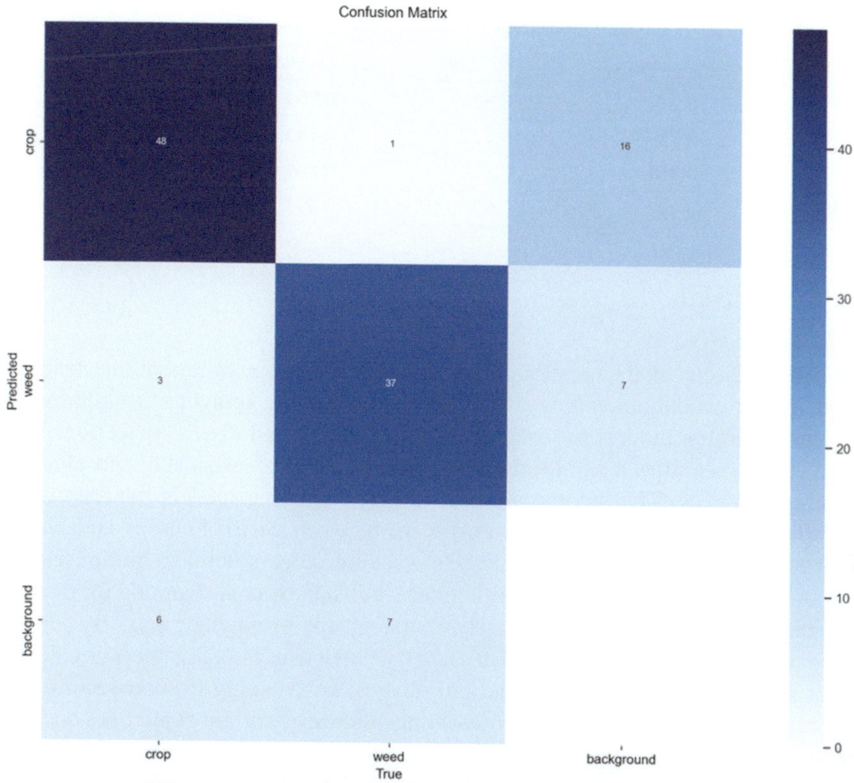

Fig. 4 Confusion matrix

Fig. 5 Disease detection

Table 2 Comparison of tested algorithms

	Accuracy	F1 score	Precision	Recall
SVM	0.917	0.894	0.903	0.89
k-NN	0.78	0.727	0.742	0.724
FCNN	0.914	0.892	0.899	0.892
CNN	0.993	0.99	0.991	0.99

7 Conclusion

This paper discusses the creation of a sophisticated agricultural robot that features modules for seeding, weeding, irrigation, and pesticide spraying, in addition to machine learning models for crop-weed classification and disease detection. This development signifies a significant advancement towards sustainable and efficient farming practices. The incorporation of machine learning models for crop-weed classification empowers the robot to discern between desirable crops and weeds accurately. This not only streamlines the weeding process but also minimises the risk of unintended crop damage. Furthermore, utilising machine learning for disease detection in plants provides a proactive strategy for managing crops. By identifying and responding to potential diseases in their early stages, the agricultural robot aids in preventing widespread crop losses, contributing to food security. In essence, this comprehensive agrobot not only addresses current challenges such as labour shortages and imprecise resource management but also future proofs agriculture by incorporating intelligent technologies. By merging robotics and machine learning, this solution paves the way for a more resilient, sustainable, and technologically advanced agricultural sector, fostering increased yields, economic viability for farmers, and a positive environmental impact. As we navigate the complexities of modern agriculture, the agrobot emerges as a key enabler in the quest for a more efficient, productive, and sustainable future for Indian farming.

References

1. Lagad S, Karmore S (2017) Design and development of agrobot for pesticide spraying using grading system. In: 2017 International conference of electronics, communication and aerospace technology (ICECA), vol 2, pp 279–283
2. Prajith AS, Nowfiya BS, Noushad N, Muhammed Ashik S, Subi S, Dhinu Lal M (2020) Automatic agricultural robot—Agrobot. In: 2020 IEEE Bangalore humanitarian technology conference (B-HTC), pp 1–5
3. Sowjanya KD, Sindhu R, Parijatham M, Srikanth K, Bhargav P (2017) Multipurpose autonomous agricultural robot. In: 2017 International conference of electronics, communication and aerospace technology (ICECA), vol 2, pp 696–699
4. Fan Z, Qiu Q, Meng Z (2017) Implementation of a four-wheel drive agricultural mobile robot for crop/soil information collection on the open field. In: 2017 32nd Youth academic annual conference of Chinese association of automation (YAC). IEEE, pp 408–412

5. Liu J, Wang X (2021) Plant diseases and pests detection based on deep learning: a review. Plant Methods 17:1–18
6. Zhao L, Li S (2020) Object detection algorithm based on improved YOLOv3. Electronics 9(3):537
7. Prajith AS, Nowfiya BS, Noushad N, Muhammed Ashik S, Subi S, Dhinu Lal M (2020) Automatic agricultural robot—Agrobot. In: 2020 IEEE Bangalore humanitarian technology conference (B-HTC). Vijiyapur, India, pp 1–5. https://doi.org/10.1109/B-HTC50970.2020.9297922
8. Beeharry Y, Bassoo V (2020) Performance of ANN and AlexNet for weed detection using UAV-based images. In: 2020 3rd International conference on emerging trends in electrical, electronic and communications engineering (ELECOM), pp 163–167
9. Elstone L, How KY, Brodie S, Ghazali MZ, Heath WP, Grieve B (2020) High speed crop and weed identification in lettuce fields for precision weeding. Sensors 20(2) [Online]. Available: https://www.mdpi.com/1424-8220/20/2/455
10. Dharanika T, Karthik SR, Vel SS, Vyaas S, Yogeshwaran S (2021) Automatic leaf disease identification and fertilizer agrobot. In: 2021 7th International conference on advanced computing and communication systems (ICACCS), vol 1. IEEE, pp 1341–1344
11. Elstone L, How KY, Brodie S, Ghazali MZ, Heath WP, Grieve B (2020) High speed crop and weed identification in lettuce fields for precision weeding. Sensors 20(2):455
12. Praseena S, Sanjena S, Thejaswini S, Selvi DMS (2019) Sensor based agrobot for sowing seeds [Online]. Available: https://api.semanticscholar.org/CorpusID:213181567
13. Karthikeyan M, Manimegalai D (2022) Automatic soil moisture control and seed sowing using agrobot. In: 2022 2nd International conference on advance computing and innovative technologies in engineering (ICACITE), pp 375–379
14. Balaji B, Shivakumara M, Sunil Y, Yamuna A, Shruthi M (2018) Smart phone operated multipurpose agricultural robot. Int J Eng Res Technol 7(05):478–481
15. Shivaprasad K, Wadhawan A (2023) Deep learning-based plant leaf disease detection. In: 2023 7th International conference on intelligent computing and control systems (ICICCS), pp 360–365

Intelligent Fall Detection Vest with Integrated Airbag System for Elderly Safety

Anne Staicy Philip, Albin Sunil Skaria, Angith S. Menon, C. K. Hariprasad, and Reshma Jose

Abstract Falls in the elderly pose a serious threat to their health and well-being, often leading to serious injuries and loss of independence. To address this urgent concern, this project introduces a smart vest with an advanced fall detection mechanism and an integrated airbag deployment system. The fall detection mechanism is based on a fall detection algorithm using accelerometer sensors. These sensors detect precise changes in direction and velocity and can pinpoint fall patterns. Upon detecting a fall event, the sensor activates a relay module, which subsequently triggers a solenoid valve. This valve controls the flow of air to DC air pumps, inflating swim tubes strategically placed around the chest and waist regions of the vest. This rapid response aims to cushion the impact of falls, significantly reducing the risk of serious injury. Parallel to the inflation process, caregivers are promptly notified of the fall event through a dedicated mobile application. The main goal is to detect falls promptly and deploy airbags within the vest to cushion the impact and minimize the risk of serious injury. This project emphasizes user-centered design to ensure the comfort and inconspicuousness of vests worn daily by the elderly. Emphasizing user comfort, the system aims to proactively mitigate fall-related injuries among the elderly, revolutionizing elderly care by offering timely protection and enhancing independence and safety, ultimately improving their quality of life. Connecting this technology with health monitoring systems ensures immediate assistance post-fall. Further evolution includes integrating this system into various wearable devices, prioritizing user comfort and aesthetics for widespread adoption. By integrating advanced technology with a user- friendly design, this fall detection vest offers a proactive solution to mitigate the impact of falls and enhance the quality of life.

Keywords Fall detection · Geriatric safety · Accelerometer sensor

A. S. Philip (✉) · A. S. Skaria · A. S. Menon · C. K. Hariprasad · R. Jose
Department of Biomedical Engineering, Sahrdaya College of Engineering and Technology, Kodakara, Thrissur, Kerala, India
e-mail: annestaicyt@gmail.com

R. Jose
e-mail: reshmajose@sahrdaya.ac.in

G. K. Rajanikant and P. Pré (eds.), *Perspectives on Global Transformation*, Lecture Notes in Electrical Engineering 1368, https://doi.org/10.1007/978-981-96-6707-9_5

1 Introduction

As the global population ages, ensuring the safety and well-being of elderly individuals becomes an increasingly pressing concern. Falls among the elderly pose a significant risk to their health and independence, necessitating innovative solutions for timely detection and prevention. In the realm of fall detection technologies, the integration of various sensors [1] and advanced algorithms has become instrumental in enhancing the accuracy and effectiveness of detection mechanisms. Machine learning algorithms, a stalwart in the technological landscape [2], play a pivotal role in fall detection by scrutinizing sensor data and discerning patterns [3] associated with falls. Through continuous refinement with large datasets, these algorithms evolve to achieve heightened accuracy, minimizing false positives and enhancing the reliability of fall detection systems [4]. Signal processing techniques constitute another cornerstone in the arsenal of fall detection methodologies. By dissecting sensor data using methods like time-domain analysis, frequency-domain analysis, and wavelet analysis, these techniques extract crucial features that signal a potential fall event. This approach delves into the intricacies of sensor data, offering a nuanced understanding of the pattern's indicative of a fall.

Infrared arrays bring a thermal dimension to fall detection, detecting changes in temperature and pinpointing the location of an individual within space. The fusion of infrared data with other sensor inputs [5] enriches the detection algorithms, enabling a more comprehensive understanding of fall- related events. Ultrasonic sensors, by measuring distance variations over time, contribute to the tapestry of fall detection technologies. These sensors capture changes in proximity, allowing algorithms to identify patterns associated with a fall event. This approach offers a unique perspective, particularly in environments where visual cues might be limited. Vision-based systems, leveraging cameras [6] to monitor changes in posture and body shape, represent an evolving frontier in fall detection [7]. Analyzing video data enables algorithms to recognize distinct patterns indicative of a fall event, offering a complementary approach to sensor-based methodologies.

The integration of accelerometer sensors in wearable devices [8] for fall detection, coupled with an advanced airbag system, represents a transformative advancement in elderly safety technology. These sensors, adept at capturing changes in acceleration and orientation, feed detailed data to sophisticated algorithms [9] that discern precise fall patterns. The synergy between these sensors and an immediate-response airbag system ensures a swift and customized deployment upon detecting a fall event, reducing the risk of serious injuries. The user-centered design, emphasizing comfort and inconspicuous wear, promotes regular use. The holistic approach, combining detection accuracy with rapid response, not only enhances fall prevention but also contributes to a comprehensive solution that prioritizes well-being and independence of the elderly.

2 Design and Methodology

2.1 Design

During the design phase using Blender software, the vest drew inspiration from the structural framework of a firefighter's jacket [8]. Modifications were subsequently introduced, featuring a dedicated square compartment housing the triggering mechanism for the airbag system. The innovation continued with the creation of the airbag itself, ingeniously crafted into two distinct compartments. One of these compartments enveloped the neck area, while the other was strategically positioned around the waist region [10]. This design enhancement was meticulously aimed at optimizing the airbag system's efficiency by ensuring its placement in critical areas of the body, thereby enhancing the distribution and effectiveness of the protective mechanism. The comprehensive design aims to offer enhanced safety and protection while integrating seamlessly into the vest's structure (Fig. 1).

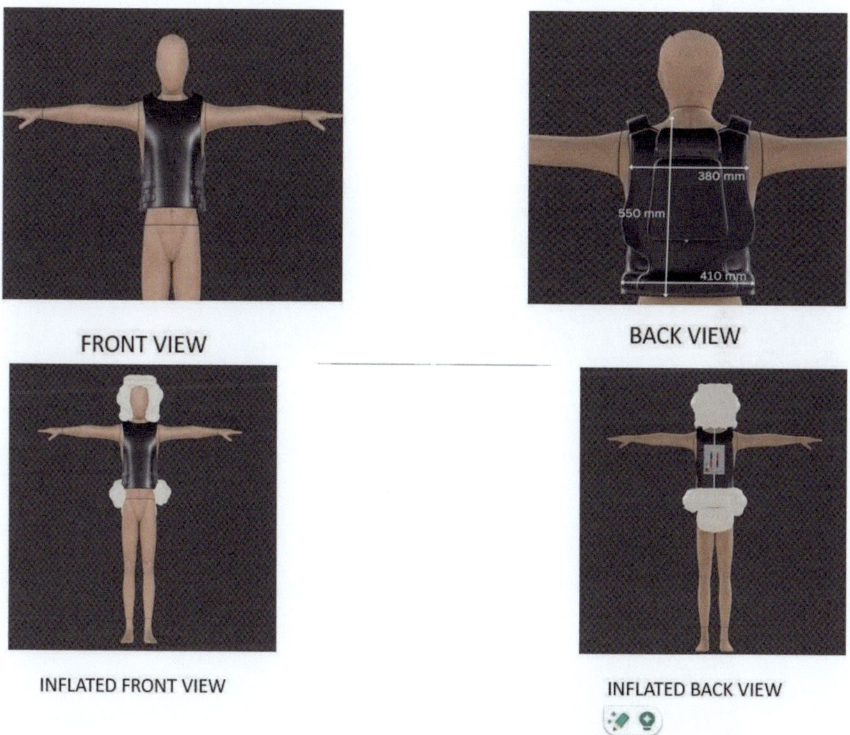

Fig. 1 Design of vest

2.2 Methodology

The vest has been meticulously designed through the adaptation of firefighter jackets, incorporating a specialized compartment to house the Inflation module components. When the wearer of the jacket experiences discomfort or displays angular posture variations beyond a predefined threshold value, these deviations are detected. The system promptly transmits a signal to the ESP32 module. Using an MPU6050 sensor, the system gathers real-time data on acceleration and orientation [4]. This data is processed to detect sudden changes indicative of a fall event. If the calculated parameters exceed predefined thresholds, signaling a potential fall, the system activates the relay module. Upon activation, the relay triggers the inflation mechanism, inflating the airbag crafted from nylon fabric, the same material used in vehicles. Nylon, a synthetic polymer classified under polyamides, is recognized for its strength, durability, and versatility. Notable properties include high tensile strength, resistance to abrasion and chemicals, elasticity, and low moisture absorption compared to other fibers. There are different types, such as Nylon 6 with six carbon atoms and Nylon 66 derived from adipic acid and hexamethylene diamine, both containing six carbon atoms. This inflation occurs through a series of controlled actions, including the activation of solenoid valves and DC pumps (Fig. 2).

To ensure the safety and comfort of the wearer, a DPST switch allows for manual control over the inflation process. This switch enables the wearer or caregiver to initiate or halt inflation as needed, providing an additional layer of control and safety. Furthermore, the system incorporates a mobile application to alert caregivers in real

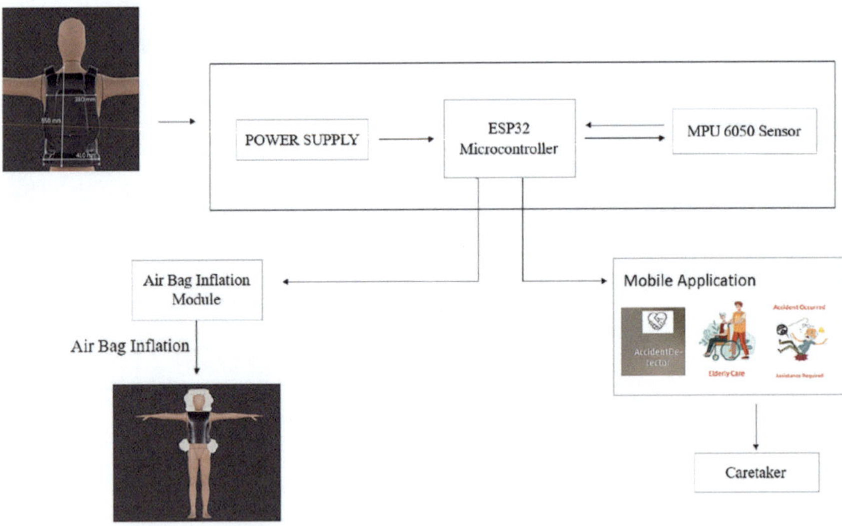

Fig. 2 Block diagram of system

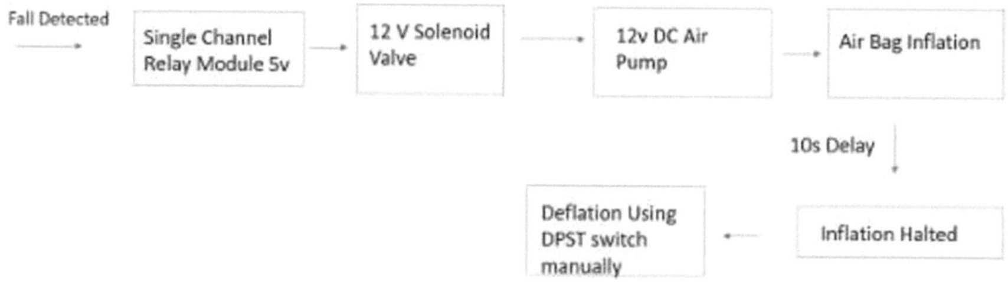

Fig. 3 Block diagram of inflation module

time about fall events detected by the vest [9]. This immediate notification ensures prompt assistance and intervention, enhancing overall safety and well-being.

2.2.1 Inflation Module

The innovation extended to the creation of the airbag itself, which was ingeniously designed with a compartment housing the triggering mechanism for the airbag system. This compartment is equipped with the necessary components, including Six DC12Vair pumps, a single-channel relay module (powered by 5 V), a 12 V solenoid valve, a 12 V 4.2Ah battery, a DPST switch, and two swim tubes. The 12 V 4.2Ah battery serves as the primary power source for the entire system, with the DPST switch acting as the main power switch to control the system's operation. When the DPST switch is turned on, power is supplied to all components, initiating the system's readiness. In operation, Six DC 12 V air pumps rapidly inflate the airbag once triggered [11], drawing power from the battery through the DPST switch. A single-channel relay module, powered by a 5 V source, is responsible for controlling the solenoid valve, which releases the compressed air into the airbag. This relay module is connected to a fall detection sensor or system. When a fall is detected, the sensor sends a signal to the relay module, activating the solenoid valve to release air from the pumps into the airbag. The two swim tubes serve as the airbag, connected to both the air pumps and the solenoid valve. When the solenoid valve opens, the air pumps inflate the tubes, rapidly deploying the airbag around the wearer to cushion the fall. During normal operation, the DPST switch is turned off, ensuring the system remains inactive and the airbag remains deflated, conserving power. However, upon detecting a fall, the DPST switch is activated, supplying power to the system. This triggers the fall detection sensor, which sends a signal to the relay module. The relay module then swiftly activates the solenoid valve, releasing the compressed air from the pumps into the swim tubes. This rapid inflation deploys the airbag around the wearer, providing cushioning thereby reducing the risk of injuries (Fig. 3).

3 Result

3.1 Air Bag Inflation Using Chemical Reaction

The reaction between sodium azide (NaN_3) and potassium nitrate (KNO_3) to produce nitrogen gas (N_2) is typically initiated by a high-temperature treatment or spark. This reaction is often utilized in automotive airbag systems [12] where the rapid generation of nitrogen gas causes the airbag to inflate. Silicon dioxide (SiO_2) can act as a suppressor by absorbing or preventing the buildup of excessive heat, thereby inhibiting the reaction between sodium azide and potassium nitrate. When silicon dioxide is introduced to the reaction mixture, it acts as a heat sink or suppressor. Silicon dioxide has high thermal stability and can absorb heat efficiently. It prevents the buildup of excessive heat required to initiate the reaction between sodium azide and potassium nitrate, thereby inhibiting the rapid generation of nitrogen gas. By altering the molecular ratios of sodium azide and potassium nitrate, the rate of nitrogen gas production can be controlled. Different ratios would affect the number of reactants available for the reaction, ultimately impacting the rate and extent of nitrogen gas formation. However, the specific ratios used in airbag systems are generally optimized and standardized for safety and performance reasons. Table 1 shows the reaction occurred in different molecular ratios and it is understood on the impact of concentration of silicon dioxide should be kept in a controlled ratio such that the reaction should not be suppressed.

While using a chemical reaction of sodium azide and potassium nitrate for airbag inflation offers some benefits, such as rapid deployment and reliable performance, it also poses significant disadvantages and safety concerns, especially in the context of a wearable device like a fall detection vest. One major disadvantage is the inherent risk associated with sodium azide. Sodium azide is highly toxic and can be explosive under certain conditions. Handling and storing sodium azide require strict precautions to prevent accidental exposure, which could pose serious health risks to both users and caregivers. In the event of a malfunction or leakage within the inflation mechanism, exposure to sodium azide could lead to severe health consequences, including poisoning and respiratory issues. The use of sodium azide raises concerns about the potential for unintended explosions or chemical reactions within the vest. In a wearable device meant to provide protection and support to elderly individuals,

Table 1 Testing of chemical reactions in different molecular ratio

Sodium azide	Potassium nitrate	Silicon dioxide	Result
0.5	0.5	0	N_2 gas produced. Presence of spark
1.1	1.0	1.6	Reaction was suppressed
1.1	1.0	0.9	Reaction was suppressed
0.6	1	0.2	Reaction was suppressed
0.6	0.6	0.1	N_2 gas produced in a small volume

the presence of an explosive substance like sodium azide introduces an unnecessary safety risk. Accidental activation or mishandling of the inflation system could result in unintended inflation of the airbags, potentially causing harm or discomfort to the wearer. In addition to the risks associated with sodium azide, the use of a chemical reaction for airbag inflation may also compromise wearer safety in other ways. The deployment of airbags through a chemical reaction introduces complexity and uncertainty into the system, increasing the likelihood of malfunctions or failures. Any disruption to the chemical reaction process could lead to incomplete inflation or unpredictable deployment of the airbags, compromising their effectiveness in protecting the wearer during a fall event.

3.2 Air Bag Inflation Using Dc Air Pump

3.2.1 Testing and Validation

To simulate different states in individuals, tests were conducted by mimicking the rest state and simulating fall events. For the rest state, individuals were positioned in a stationary position, such as sitting or lying down, ensuring they were comfortable and relaxed. Baseline physiological parameters like heart rate, breathing rate, and body temperature were measured using devices such as ECG monitors, respiratory sensors, and thermometers. This position was maintained for a specific period, typically 10–15 min, to ensure the body was in a resting state. To simulate fall events, safety was prioritized by using cushioned surfaces and safety harnesses [7]. Individuals were equipped with accelerometers and motion capture systems to measure sudden accelerations accurately. Controlled falls were performed using mechanisms like a harness and controlled drop system or a platform that dropped suddenly, mimicking the sensation of a fall while ensuring the individual's safety. Backward falls were primarily considered in this study.

The test was mainly based on the number of DC air pumps used for inflation, where an increase in the number of pumps resulted in a decrease in inflation time and modified the threshold detection [13]. The threshold values and corresponding events are shown in Table 2, while the number of DC air pumps used, and the time taken for inflation are presented in Table 3.

Table 2 Threshold values and corresponding events

Threshold values	Event
39,000	Fall
40,000	Fall
20,000	Rest
26,000	Rest

Table 3 Number of DC air pumps used, and the time taken for inflation

No. of DC air pump used	Time taken for inflation
01	4 min
03	2 min
05	45 s
06	20 s

3.2.2 Vest Prototype and App Integration

A prototype of the vest with an integrated airbag module was successfully developed. The program for the designed algorithm was integrated and run successfully, enabling accurate fall detection, particularly for backward falls. The inflation of the airbag was completed within 20 s. Additionally, automated inflation and manual deflation features were implemented. A mobile application was successfully developed, providing alerts to caregivers and generating reports (Figs. 4, 5 and 6).

The integration of a mobile application for signal delivery to caregivers adds a layer of real-time communication to the system. The mobile app is designed to transmit relevant data and alerts to designated caretakers promptly. This feature ensures that caregivers receive immediate notifications in the event of a fall, enabling swift assistance and intervention. The seamless communication between the smart vest and the mobile application enhances the overall effectiveness of the system, promoting timely care and support for elderly individuals. The proposed smart vest not only emphasizes high accuracy in fall detection through advanced sensors and algorithms but also introduces an innovative airbag system for impact prevention. The integration of a mobile application adds an extra dimension to the system, facilitating swift communication with caregivers for immediate assistance. These combined features underscore the potential of the system to significantly improve the safety and well-being of elderly individuals by providing accurate, rapid, and preventive measures in the face of fall-related incidents.

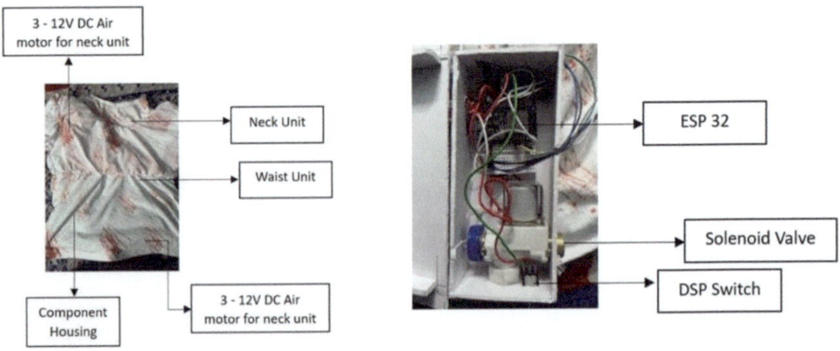

Fig. 4 Prototype and component housing

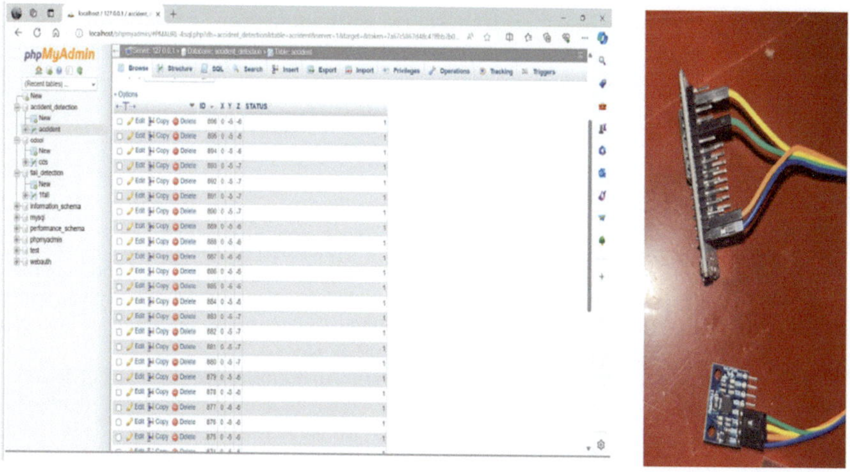

Fig. 5 Real-time data stored in MySQL server and sensors

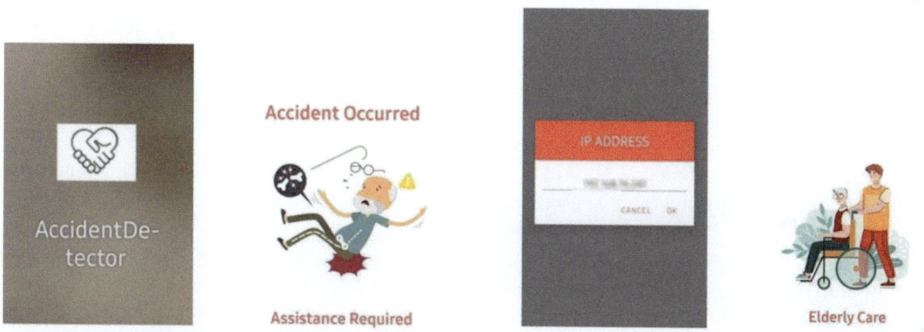

Fig. 6 App interface

4 Conclusion

In conclusion, the intelligent fall detection vest with an integrated airbag system represents a groundbreaking solution to mitigate the critical issue of fall-related injuries among the elderly [14]. Precise sensor technology, chemical reactions for rapid airbag inflation, and the incorporation of a microcontroller unit demonstrate a holistic approach to enhancing safety and independence. The emphasis on user-centered design ensures seamless integration into daily life, promising not only protection but an improved quality of life for the elderly. Future developments for enhancing a fall detection vest include implementing advanced inflation mechanisms to significantly reduce inflation time, thus improving user comfort and response time during fall detection [12]. Utilizing nylon material and ergonomic design principles will enhance comfort, durability, and adaptability of the vest. Exploring innovative battery technologies or optimizing current designs to decrease the battery's weight will improve portability and usability without compromising performance or safety. Refining fall detection algorithms to prioritize detection accuracy for forward and lateral falls will address common scenarios of concern, enhancing the overall effectiveness of fall detection.

References

1. Werner F, Diermaier J, Schmid S, Panek P (2011) Fall detection with distributed floor- mounted accelerometers: an overview of the development and evaluation of a fall detection system within the project ehome. In: 2011 5th international conference on pervasive computing technologies for healthcare (PervasiveHealth) and workshops. IEEE, pp 354–361
2. Khan MS, Yu M, Feng P, Wang L, Chambers J (2015) An unsupervised acoustic fall detection system using source separation for sound interference suppression. Signal Process 110:199–210
3. Zigel Y, Litvak D, Gannot I (2009) A method for automatic fall detection of elderly people using floor vibrations and sound—proof of concept on human mimicking doll falls. IEEE Trans Biomed Eng 56(12):2858–2867
4. He Y, Li Y, Bao SD (2012) Fall detection by built-in tri-accelerometer of smartphone. In: Proceedings of 2012 IEEE-EMBS international conference on biomedical and health informatics. IEEE, pp 184–187
5. Chen Z, Wang Y (2018) Infrared–ultrasonic sensor fusion for support vector machine–based fall detection. J Intell Mater Syst Struct 29(9):2027–2039
6. Albawendi S, Appiah K, Powell H, Lotfi A (2016) Video based fall detection with enhanced motion history images. In: Proceedings of the 9th ACM international conference on pervasive technologies related to assistive environments, p 17
7. Tran T-H, Le T L, Hoang V-N, Vu H (2017) Continuous detection of human fall using multimodal features from kinect sensors in scalable environment. Comput Methods Programs Biomed 146:151–165
8. Nyan M, Tay FE, Manimaran M, Seah K (2006) Garment-based detection of falls and activities of daily living using 3-axis mems accelerometer. J Phys Conf Ser 34(1):1059. IOP Publishing
9. Habib MA, Mohktar MS, Kamaruzzaman SB, Lim KS, Pin TM, Ibrahim F (2014) Smartphone-based solutions for fall detection and prevention: challenges and open issues. Sensors 14(4):7181–7208
10. Tamura T, Yoshimura T, Sekine M, Uchida M, Tanaka O (2009) A wearable airbag to prevent fall injuries. IEEE Trans Inf Technol Biomed 13(6):910–914
11. Thella AK, Suryadevara VK, Rizkalla M, Hossain G (2016) Smart unit care for pre fall detection and prevention. In: 2016 IEEE national aerospace and electronics conference (NAECON) and Ohio Innovation Summit (OIS). IEEE, pp 220–224
12. Shi G, Chan CS, Li WJ, Leung K-S, Zou Y, Jin Y (2009) Mobile human airbag system for fall protection using mems sensors and embedded svm classifier. IEEE Sens J 9(5):495–503
13. Kostopoulos P, Kyritsis AI, Deriaz M, Konstantas D (2016) F2d: A location aware fall detection system tested with real data from daily life of elderly people. Procedia Comput Sci 98:212–219
14. Demura S, Kasuga K, Sato S, Sato T, Shin S (2013) Determination of persons at a high risk of falling in a population of healthy community-dwelling elderly japanese. Int J Gerontol 7(1):13–16
15. Trofimova AA, Masciadri A, Veronese F, Salice F (2017) Indoor human detection based on thermal array sensor data and adaptive background estimation. J Comput Commun 5(4):16–28

Efficient Maximum and Minimum Finding Circuits for Machine Learning Applications

P. Shareefa Fairoose and Ashutosh Mishra

Abstract This paper presents efficient maximum and minimum computing architecture that can be used in Machine learning applications like the max pooling layer, SoftMax activation function, Morphological operations, etc. Proposed architecture is implemented using Verilog and tested using the vivado test bench. Design synthesis is performed using Cadence Genus, TSMC 90 nm technology node. The results show that the proposed Maximum computing architecture has achieved a 36.07% reduction in Area-Delay-Product (ADP) with a 7.63% increment in Power-Delay-Product (PDP), and the proposed minimum computing circuit has achieved a 45.09% reduction in ADP and a 26.52% reduction in PDP compared with (Zhang in Electronics (Switzerland) 10:10, 2021.). New algorithms for handling signed inputs are proposed. Pro-posed signed circuits have a slight increment in ADP and PDP compared to unsigned circuits, it is due to the extra circuit necessary to handle signed inputs.

Keywords Morphological operations · Machine learning applications · SoftMax activation function · Area-delay-product (ADP) · Power-delay-product (PDP)

1 Introduction

Maximum and minimum computing circuits are required by many applications, like Machine learning [1, 2], Morphological operations [3], and image and signal processing applications. The maximum and minimum computing methods proposed in [4] designed for the systolic array architecture. Zhang [5] proposed maximum and minimum computing by logic operations instead of comparators and delay elements. The proposed architecture in [5] reduces hardware resources for grayscale morphological operations. We modified this architecture for signed numbers input. These

P. Shareefa Fairoose (✉) · A. Mishra
Department of ECE, NIT Calicut, Kozhikode, India
e-mail: shareefa_p210133ec@nitc.ac.in

A. Mishra
e-mail: ashutosh@nitc.ac.in

G. K. Rajanikant and P. Pré (eds.), *Perspectives on Global Transformation*, Lecture Notes in Electrical Engineering 1368, https://doi.org/10.1007/978-981-96-6707-9_6

can be used for machine learning applications like max-pooling, SoftMax, etc. In this paper, we modified the circuit given in [5] to reduce the delay along with reduced ADP and PDP. We modified the circuit to take 4 inputs at a time and five such architectures are used to implement a maximum/minimum computing unit for 16 inputs. This architecture is designed for maximum computing unit in SoftMax function, which is used at the first stage of the implementation on FPGA, to prevent overflow. This similar idea can be extended to other applications according to the number of inputs it takes. Architecture proposed in [6] take 16 inputs parallelly and processing with 16 parallel units is the best for getting less ADP while implementing SoftMax on FPGA. We have also included signed logic for signed inputs since ML computations use signed numbers. The proposed circuits for maximum and minimum computing in [5] are for unsigned numbers. We have proposed modified architecture for finding the maximum/minimum among 16 unsigned numbers.

Remaining paper is arranged as; Sect. 2 explains the proposed architecture, Sect. 3 explains its VLSI implementation results and comparison with available literature followed by the conclusions in Sect. 4.

2 Maximum and Minimum Computing Circuits

2.1 Unsigned Maximum and Minimum Computing Circuit

The algorithm proposed in [5] is used here for the 4-input maximum/minimum computation. The architecture is implemented using AND-OR combinations in with two input multiplexers as in Figs. 1 and 2 and gives better performance.

Figure 3 shows the block diagram of computing the min/max among 16 numbers. The 16 inputs are divided into 4 groups and applied to the M1, M2, M3, and M4 respectively. 4 outputs are available from level 1 and these 4 outputs are fed to the M5 to obtained max or min value. The proposed circuits do the operation through multiple paths. So, the critical path delay is reduced hence improvement in ADP. This idea can be extended to different combinations of max/min computing circuits according to the number of inputs.

Signed Maximum and Minimum Computing Circuit. Machine learning applications generally require signed operations. Algorithms 1 and 2 extend the proposed unsigned max/min finding circuits to handle signed inputs. In the algorithm, N = 8, is the bit width of inputs, and M = 16 represents the number of inputs. Algorithm 1 performs signed Maximum computation. The first operation is bitwise AND of all MSBs of the inputs. If it is zero, there is at least one positive number and one among those positive numbers will be a maximum value. In this case, make all negative numbers zero and other numbers remain as such and are stored in the z_i register. If all inputs are negative, the bit-wise AND operation of MSBs will be '1'. For this case, save inputs to z_i, the unsigned 16-input Max finder finds the maximum among them. The value received in the register z_i is passed to the proposed 16-input unsigned maximum computing circuit which gives the maximum among signed inputs.

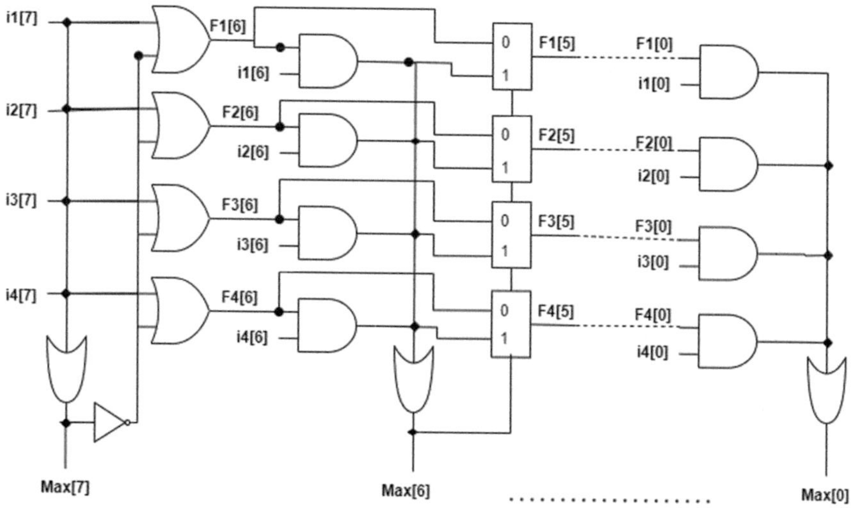

Fig. 1 4-input unsigned maximum computing circuit

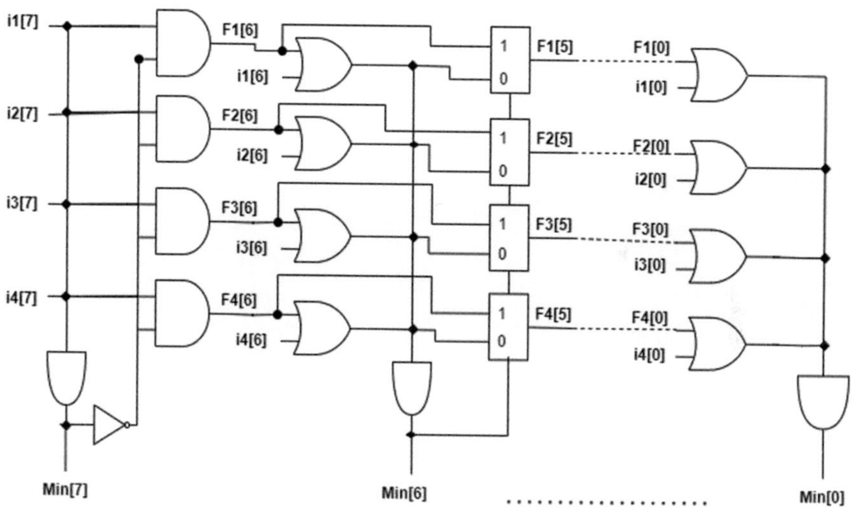

Fig. 2 4-input unsigned minimum computing circuit

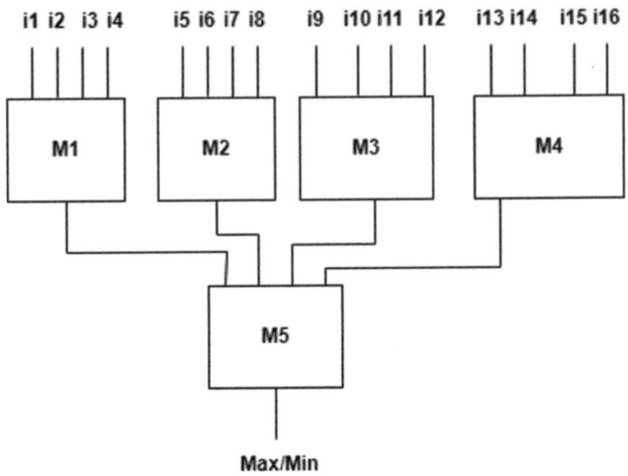

Fig. 3 16-input unsigned maximum/minimum computing circuit

Algorithm 1 Signed Maximum Computing

Input: xi (i = 1, 2,..., M) (M = 16)
Output: [N − 1: 0] y (N = 8)
Reg zi (i = 1, 2,..., M), [M − 1: 0]I
for i = M: 1 **do**
    I[i − 1] = xi [N − 1]
end for
w1 = &I
if w1 = = 1′ b1 **then** zi = xi
else
    for i = M: 1 **do**
    zi = I[i − 1] ? 8′ b0: xi
end for
end if
unsigned maximum finder dut1(zi, y)

Algorithm 2 Signed Minimum Computing

Input: xi (i = 1, 2,..., M) (M = 16)
Output: [N − 1: 0] y (N = 8)
Reg zi (i = 1, 2,..., M), [M − 1: 0]I
for i = M: 1 **do**
    I[i − 1] = xi [N − 1]
end for
w1 = |I
if w1 = = 1′ b0 **then** zi = xi
else
    for i = M: 1 **do**
    zi = I[i − 1] ? xi: 8’hff
end for
end if
unsigned minimum finder dut1(zi, y)

Similarly, Algorithm 2 performs minimum computing operation among 16 signed numbers. This same idea can be applied to perform signed Max/Min computation of any number of inputs. In the signed minimum computing circuit, bit-wise OR operation of all MSBs of input is performed. If output is zero, inputs are passed to the z_i register as it is. If the output is one, all positive inputs, hexadecimal FF, and negative numbers pass as it is to the z_i register. Finally, the z_i register gives input to the 16-input unsigned minimum computing circuit that gives signed minimum output.

3 VLSI Implementation Results

Proposed designs and previous designs in [5] for 16 inputs are implemented using Verilog and tested using vivado test bench. Synthesis is performed by Cadence genus, using TSMC 90-nm CMOS cell library. Synthesis results are listed in Tables 1 and 2. Both Proposed unsigned 16-input Max and Min computing circuits have less ADP compared to that proposed in [5]. A 16-input Max computing circuit has a 36.07% ADP reduction compared to that proposed in [5]. Similarly, an unsigned minimum computing circuit has obtained an ADP reduction of 45.09% to that in [5]. The PDP of the proposed un-signed Maximum finding circuit is increased by 7.63%. The PDP of the proposed minimum computing circuit is decreased by 26.52%. ADP and PDP of the signed Min and Max computing circuits are shown in Table 2. Signed circuits have some increment in ADP and PDP compared to the proposed unsigned circuits due to the extra logic required to make it signed.

Table 1 Comparison of unsigned 16-input Max/Min circuits

Max/Min finder	Area (μm^2)	Power (nW)	Delay (ps)	ADP ($\mu m^2 \mu s$)	ADP reduction	PDP (nW μs)	PDP reduction
Max finder [2]	1197.416	30,784.275	4011	4.802		123.475	
Min finder [2]	1212.554	35,213.163	3878	4.702		136.556	
Proposed max finder	1416.16	61,301.385	2168	3.07	– 36.07%	132.901	+ 7.63%
Proposed min finder	1378.315	53,540.929	1874	2.582	– 45.09%	100.335	– 26.52%

Table 2 Implementation results of 16-input signed max/min finder circuits

Max/Min finder	Area (μm^2)	Power (nW)	Delay (ps)	ADP ($\mu m^2 \mu s$)	PDP (nW μs)
Proposed max finder	1580.407	80,653.162	3263	5.156	263.171
Proposed min finder	1560.728	72,158.545	3089	4.821	222.897

4 Conclusion

This paper proposes 16-input signed and unsigned maximum and minimum computing circuits. It has obtained a 36.07% reduction in ADP for an unsigned maximum computation and a 45.09% reduction in ADP for an unsigned minimum computing circuit. Signed Maximum and Minimum computing circuits can be applied in Machine Learning and image processing applications. This idea can be extended to any number of input cases according to the requirement. Signed maximum and minimum computing circuits have some increments in ADP and PDP compared to that of proposed unsigned maximum and minimum computing circuits. This is due to the extra circuitry required to make the unsigned circuit into a signed one.

References

1. Li Z, Li H, Jiang X, Chen B, Zhang Y, Du G (2018) Efficient FPGA implementation of softmax function for DNN applications. In: 2018 12th IEEE international conference on anti-counterfeiting, security, and identification (ASID). IEEE, pp 212–216
2. Hong E, Choi KA, Joo J (2023) Efficient two-stage max-pooling engines for an FPGA-based convolutional neural network. Electronics 12(19):4043
3. Nakagawa Y (1978) A note on the use of local min and max operations in digital picture processing. IEEE Trans Syst Man Cybern 8(8):632–635
4. Diamantaras KI, Kung S-Y (1997) A linear systolic array for real-time morphological image processing. J VLSI Signal Process Syst Signal Image Video Technol 17(1):43–55
5. Zhang B (2021) Reconfigurable morphological processor for grayscale image processing. Electronics (Switzerland) 10(10)
6. Wei Z, Arora A, Patel P, John L (2020) Design space exploration for softmax implemen-tations. Institute of Electrical and Electronics Engineers Inc., vol 7, pp 45–52

Association Between the Chirality of a Filament and the Helicity of the Supporting Active Regions

P. T. Jain Jacob and Ram Ajor Maurya

Abstract We investigate the handedness in the solar magnetic structures like chromospheric filaments and photospheric active regions using observations obtained from GONG, KSO and SDO/HMI. At its initial stage near the east limb, we identified a right-bearing sense for the filament barbs and negative helicity in the supporting active region (AR) NOAA 11959. Subsequently, we observed an emergence of positive helicity in this AR and a change in the bearing sense of the associated filament. Following this emergence, the filament adhered to the hemispheric helicity rule, maintaining the helicity of the underlying AR throughout its disc passage and following to the conservation of helicity. Our conclusion is that the AR in the photosphere and the filament in the chromosphere are interconnected, exhibiting similar pattern of helicity for a long duration of their lifespans.

Keywords Active regions · Helicity · Magnetic fields · Prominences

1 Introduction

Solar filaments are chromospheric magnetic structures with a lifetime ranging from a few hours to several days. They are categorized as quiescent, intermediate, or active region filaments based on the presence of active regions at their footpoints at the photosphere. They manifest two types of magnetic structures: sheared arcades and flux ropes [1]. The plasma within the filaments, defying gravity, is supported by these magnetic structures, with their spine observed along a line known as the Polarity Inversion Line (PIL), where positive and negative polarities cancel each other out. Additionally, there are segments or fragments that detach from the filament's spine on the solar surface, known as filament barbs. These detached segments resemble the legs of a caterpillar and connect with patches of minority polarity flux on either side

P. T. Jain Jacob (✉) · R. A. Maurya
Department of Physics, National Institute of Technology Calicut, Kozhikode, Kerala, India
e-mail: jain_p180130ph@nitc.ac.in

R. A. Maurya
e-mail: ramajor@nitc.ac.in

G. K. Rajanikant and P. Pré (eds.), *Perspectives on Global Transformation*, Lecture Notes in Electrical Engineering 1368, https://doi.org/10.1007/978-981-96-6707-9_7

of the PIL [2]. These barbs directly help us identify the handedness of the filament's structure. On the other hand, the handedness of the field lines in an active region can be estimated from the observations of the vector magnetic field at the photosphere.

The magnetic helicity (**H**) of an active region is defined as the volume integral of the scalar product of the magnetic vector potential (**A**) and magnetic field ($\mathbf{B} = \nabla \times \mathbf{A}$) [3].

$$\mathbf{H} = \int_V \mathbf{A} \cdot \mathbf{B}\, \mathrm{dV} \tag{1}$$

The estimation of magnetic helicity requires the values of **A** and **B** in a volume. But, observations provide magnetic field information only at the solar photospheric height. However, the photospheric magnetic field can be assumed as a force-free magnetic field to estimate the handedness in the AR, as follows,

$$\nabla \times \mathbf{B} = \alpha \mathbf{B} \tag{2}$$

where, α is the force-free parameter. It acts as a proxy for the magnetic helicity [3]. The sign of force-free parameter determined from Eq. (2) can reveal whether the AR follows a positive helicity or negative helicity. According to hemispheric helicity rule [4], ARs exhibit a positive magnetic helicity in southern hemisphere and negative helicity in northern hemisphere.

Chirality is another proxy of magnetic helicity. Solar features such as solar filaments, sunspot whorls, and coronal cavities also exhibit magnetic helicity, which can be determined by analyzing the chirality of these structures [5]. There are two kinds of chiralities: dextral and sinistral. A dextral filament has negative helicity, while a sinistral filament has positive helicity. Filaments are classified based on the dominant bearing sense, assuming they have a flux rope structure [6, 7]. Dextral filaments have more right-bearing barbs than left-bearing barbs, and vice versa [8]. Filaments follow the hemispheric helicity rule similar to ARs, meaning that filaments in the northern hemisphere have dextral chirality, while those in the southern hemisphere have sinistral chirality [9, 10].

The chirality of a filament can predict the helicity of the associated AR [11]. Directly estimating the helicity of an AR is not possible. However, the force-free parameter and chirality of associated solar features can help accurately estimate the AR's helicity. Additionally, it is possible for a positive helicity magnetic cloud to emerge from an AR of negative helicity [5]. This emergence of positive helicity near the active region, following negative helicity, can contribute to the helicity of the magnetic cloud. Studying the emergence of magnetic helicity associated with filament footpoints can simultaneously explain the observed helicity and chirality patterns.

The determination of bearing sense of the filaments at multiple times and examination of helicity of associated solar features can provide unambiguous estimation of helicity of solar filaments. In this study, we examined an AR filament for long duration. The simultaneous estimation of helicity in the associated ARs and bearing sense of filament helped us to validate relation between photospheric and chromospheric properties. Rest of the paper is organized as follows: In Sect. 2, we provide a description of the instrument specifications and an overview of the observations. Section 3 is dedicated to data analysis procedures and presenting the results and interpreting our observations. Finally, in Sect. 4, we provide a summary and conclusions of our findings.

2 Observational Data

We utilized observational data from ground-based observatories such as the Global Oscillation Network Group [12] (GONG) at Cerro Tololo Inter-American Observatory (CT) in Chile, the Kanzelhöehe Solar Observatory (KSO) in Austria, and the space-based observatory Solar Dynamics Observatory [13] (SDO). Full-disk Hα images from KSO and GONG/CT have pixel resolutions of $1''.02$ and $1''.0$, respectively. These data were employed to differentiate the bearing sense of the filament during January 16 to 25, 2014. Additionally, to determine the magnetic helicity of ARs, we utilized disambiguated vector magnetic field data provided by the Helioseismic and Magnetic Imager (HMI) onboard SDO, which has a pixel resolution of $0''.6$.

3 Analysis and Results

We examined the chirality and helicity of a solar filament and associated ARs (NOAA 11959 and 11960), respectively, for several days during their disc crossing. The solar filament and ARs are marked in Fig. 1c. Major results of our analysis are depicted in Figs. 1, 2, 3 and 4.

3.1 *Chirality of Filament*

We determined the chirality or bearing sense of the filament as depicted in [14]. The left and right bearing sense of a filament barb can be explained as follows: if we move along the barb towards the filament's spine and find that the barb is making an acute angle with the left side part of the spine, it will have left bearing (or sinistral), see Fig. 1a. Similarly, if the barb is making an acute angle with the right side part of the spine, it will have right bearing (or dextral), see Fig. 1b.

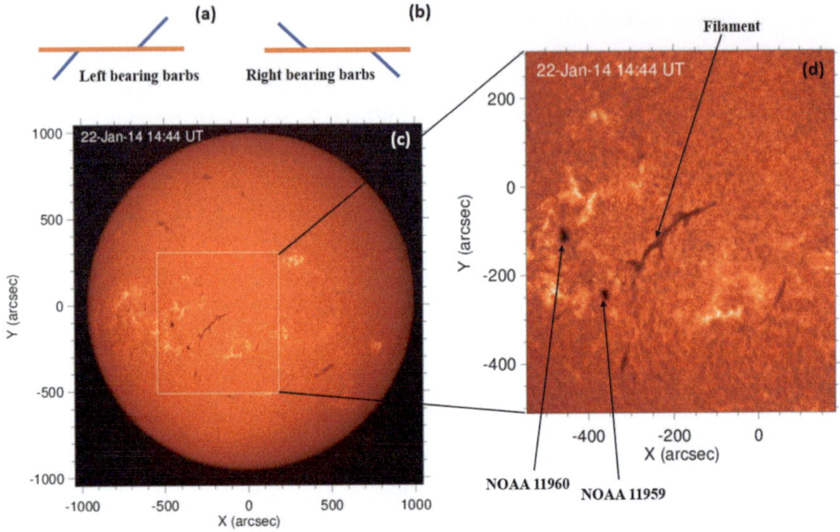

Fig. 1 The two kinds of bearing sense of barbs are plotted in panels **a** and **b** for the reference. The orange thick line and blue line segments represent the spine and barbs of filament, respectively. The panel **c** shows the KSO full-disk Hα image of Sun on 22 Jan, 2014. The white region represent the field-of-view of filament and associated ARs. The magnified image of specified region was plotted in panel **d**

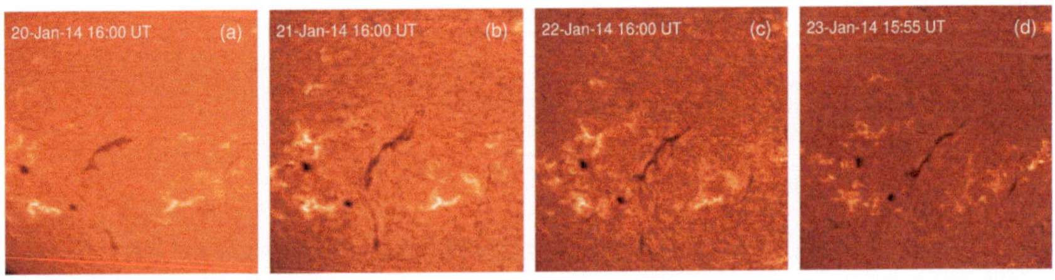

Fig. 2 The GONG/CT Hα images from the field-of-view marked in Fig. 1c. The evolution of filament and associated ARs from 20 Jan to 23 Jan was plotted

We analysed the bearing sense of the filament at four different dates of their disc passage as shown in Fig. 2. The filament exhibited a right bearing sense on its initial stages of observations as seen in Fig. 2a and classified as dextral filament during this time. We observed a change in overall bearing sense from right bearing to left bearing on 21 January (see Fig. 2b). The filament exhibited an overall left bearing sense after this. From this, the filament can be classified into sinistral filament. The filament follows the hemispheric helicity rule from 21 January. We identified left bearing sense for this filament from 22 Jan to 25 Jan, see Fig. 2c, d.

Fig. 3 The evolution of NOAA 11959 (as marked in Fig. 1d) observed in SDO/HMI from 21 Jan to 25 Jan was plotted. The white region represent the magnetic field with positive polarity

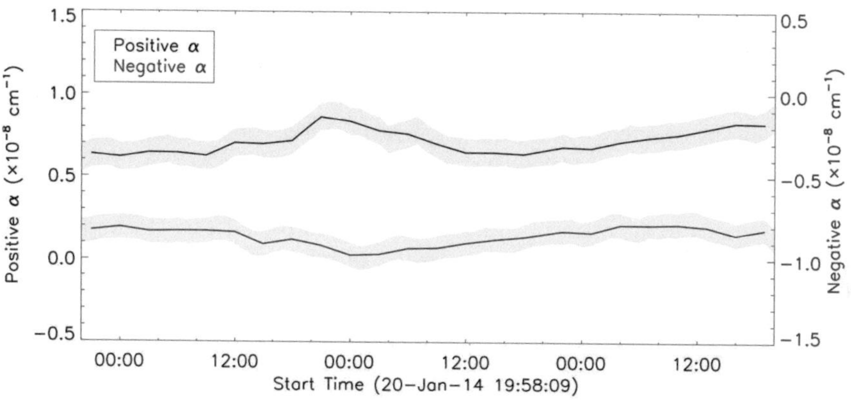

Fig. 4 The average z-component of force-free parameter of magnetic helicity obtained from NOAA 11959. The positive and negative helicity variation with respect to time are drawn in black and blue lines, respectively. The shaded regions represent the error in the calculation of the parameter α

3.2 *Helicity of Active Regions*

The force-free parameter (α) is considered as proxy of the magnetic helicity (**H**) in Eq. (1). It can be estimated using the formula [3],

$$\alpha^z(x, y) = \sum_{x,y} \frac{(\frac{\partial B_y}{\partial x} - \frac{\partial B_x}{\partial y})B_z}{B_z^2} \tag{3}$$

where B_x, B_y, and B_z represent the x, y, and z components of the magnetic field. We estimated the parameter α using Eq. (3) for NOAA 11959 and 11960. To avoid errors in helicity calculation caused by noisy magnetic fields in observations, we considered only those pixels where $|B_z| > 200G$. The total positive and negative helicity in this region (see Fig. 3) was calculated, giving more weight to pixels with larger positive and negative magnetic fields. We then compared the magnitude of total positive and negative helicity present in this region. The calculated positive and negative helicity for these regions over four days was plotted in Fig. 4.

We identified that one of the foot points of the filament was rooted in NOAA 11959. The overall magnetic helicity of this region was negative on first two days January 20th and 21st. From January 21st onwards, we observed an increase in average positive helicity and a decrease in negative helicity in this region. The temporal evolution of the magnetic helicity at NOAA 11959 is illustrated in Fig. 4. Additionally, we noted a similar pattern of temporal evolution of positive and negative helicity at NOAA 11960, which is situated on the positive polarity side of the filament.

4 Summary and Conclusions

We study the association between the magnetic properties of a filament and supporting ARs NOAA 11959 and 11960. The filament originated from NOAA 11959. Based on the one-to-one correspondence between chirality and helicity, we can attribute negative helicity to the filament with right-bearing barbs under the assumption that it adheres to a flux rope magnetic structure [9]. In other words, the filament exhibits dextral chirality during this period. The observed negative helicity of the ARs and the right-bearing orientation of the filament during the initial stages of observation suggest that both are following the same helicity pattern. However, it's noteworthy that neither the helicity of the ARs nor the filament conforms to the hemispheric helicity rule.

We found that the observed negative magnetic helicity of these ARs persisted for many days. Moreover, after some time, we observed a change in the bearing sense of this filament from right bearing to left bearing. An associated increase in positive helicity was also observed at NOAA 11959 and 11960. This shows an emergence of a magnetic cloud with positive helicity from the filament footpoint. The emergence of positive helicity from the AR changes the bearing sense of the filament rooted in it. Now, the filament has left-bearing barbs, and it is classified as a sinistral filament. It follows the hemispheric helicity rule [4]. The filament continues to follow the sinistral chirality during the observation.

According to the conservation of helicity, the sign of helicity of AR and the magnetic cloud emerging from this region should match. Our observation obeys this rule at the initial stages. After some time, the helicity of the filament changed from negative to positive, i.e., the positive helicity filament was rooted in the negative helicity AR. It contradicts the helicity conservation rule. In a previous study on a different AR filament, a positive helicity magnetic cloud was emerging from an AR with negative helicity, and a positive helicity injection at AR maintained the conservation of helicity [5]. Similarly, we observed an increase in the positive helicity at this AR. Additionally, a change in the helicity of the filament was also associated with the positive helicity injection. We conclude that the emergence of positive helicity from the AR situated at the filament footpoint can change the sign of the helicity of the filament from negative to positive.

This filament should be further monitored for a long time to understand its formation and the presence of eruptions. In addition, incorporating the properties of coronal structures associated with it can provide a clear image of its magnetic structure.

Acknowledgements The data used here are courtesy of NASA's SDO and AIA science team. This work also utilizes data from GONG and KSO. One of the authors, RAM, acknowledges support from the ISRO RESPOND project.

References

1. Gibson SE (2018) Solar prominences: theory and models. Fleshing out the magnetic skeleton. Liv Rev Solar Phys 15(1):7
2. Liewer PC, Panasenco O, Hall JR (2012) Stereoscopic analysis of the 31 August 2007 prominence eruption and coronal mass ejection. Sol Phys 282(1):201–220
3. Maurya RA, Ambastha A (2020) Magnetic and velocity field topology in active regions of descending phase of solar cycle 23. Sol Phys 295(8)
4. Hale GE (1927) The fields of force in the atmosphere of the sun. Nature 119(3002):708–714
5. Chandra R, Pariat E, Schmieder B, Mandrini CH, Uddin W (2009) How can a negative magnetic helicity active region generate a positive helicity magnetic cloud? Sol Phys 261(1):127–148
6. Hazra S, Mahajan SS, Douglas WK, Martens PCH (2018) Hemispheric preference and cyclic variation of solar filament chirality from 2000 to 2016. Astrophys J 865(2):108
7. Pevtsov AA, Balasubramaniam KS, Rogers JW (2003) Chirality of chromospheric filaments. Astrophys J 595(1):500–505
8. Guo Y, Schmieder B, Démoulin P, Wiegelmann T, Aulanier G, Török T, Bommier V (2010) Coexisting flux rope and dipped arcade sections along one solar filament. Astrophys J 714(1):343–354
9. Hao Q, Guo Y, Fang C, Chen PF, Cao WD (2016) Can we determine the filament chirality by the filament footpoint location or the barb-bearing? Res Astron Astrophys 16(1):001
10. Zhou Z, Liu R, Cheng X, Jiang C, Wang Y, Liu L, Cui J (2020) The relationship between chirality, sense of rotation, and hemispheric preference of solar eruptive filaments. Astrophys J 891(2):180
11. Lim EK, Chae J (2009) Chirality of intermediate filaments and magnetic helicity of active regions. Astrophys J 692(1):104–108
12. Harvey JW, Hill F, Hubbard RP, Kennedy JR, Leibacher JW, Pintar JA, Gilman PA, Noyes RW, Title AM, Toomre J, Ulrich RK, Bhatnagar A, Kennewell JA, Marquette W, Patrón J, Saá O, Yasukawa E (1996) The global oscillation network group (gong) project. Science 272(5266):1284–1286
13. ...Lemen JR, Title AM, Akin DJ, Boerner PF, Chou C, Drake JF, Duncan DW, Edwards CG, Friedlaender FM, Heyman GF, Hurlburt NE, Katz NL, Kushner GD, Levay M, Lindgren RW, Mathur DP, McFeaters EL, Mitchell S, Rehse RA, Schrijver CJ, Springer LA, Stern RA, Tarbell TD, Wuelser JP, Wolfson CJ, Yanari C, Bookbinder JA, Cheimets PN, Caldwell D, Deluca EE, Gates R, Golub L, Park S, Podgorski WA, Bush RI, Scherrer PH, Gummin MA, Smith P, Auker G, Jerram P, Pool P, Soufli R, Windt DL, Beardsley S, Clapp M, Lang J, Waltham N (2011) The atmospheric imaging assembly (AIA) on the solar dynamics observatory (SDO). Sol Phys 275(1–2):17–40
14. Hanaoka Y, Sakurai T (2017) Statistical study of the magnetic field orientation in solar filaments. Astrophys J 851(2):130

Investigating Coronal Loop Dynamics: Harmonic Behavior and Magnetic Field Estimation

K. Safna Banu and Ram Ajor Maurya

Abstract In this study, we investigated harmonic oscillations in a coronal loop linked to an active region NOAA 12680, triggered by a GOES M4.7 class flare on August 28, 2021. The oscillating loop was observed using the Atmospheric Imaging Assembly (AIA) aboard the Solar Dynamics Observatory, and we estimated its length to be 172 Mm. The fundamental mode oscillation has a period of 18.5 min, with harmonics occurring at 7.6 and 4.2 min. Furthermore, utilizing the length of the coronal loop and these periods, we estimated the Alfvén speed in the loop to be 300, 559, and 1012 km/s for the respective modes. Additionally, the magnetic field strength in the coronal loop was estimated to be 11 gauss.

Keywords Solar corona · Magnetic structures · Energetic events · MHD waves and oscillations

1 Introduction

Observations of oscillations and waves in the solar corona provide valuable insights into the dynamics of coronal magnetic structures such as coronal loops and jets. These oscillatory patterns offer crucial information about plasma properties and wave generation within the solar corona. Achieving this understanding has been made possible through the implementation of a tool known as coronal seismology [1, 2].

The flare induced, ejection or eruption caused kink oscillations are intensively observed and analyzed among the Magnetohydrodynamic (MHD) waves and oscillations [3]. Initially, in 2011 Aschwanden and Schrijver [4] analyzed the flare induced transverse coronal loop oscillations (TLOs) in fundamental mode with SDO/AIA observations. The observations of harmonics are first reported by Verwichte et al. [5] then later studied in detail by Andries, Moortel and Li [6–9]. For a fundamental

K. Safna Banu (✉) · R. A. Maurya
Department of Physics, National Institute of Technology Calicut, Kozhikode, Kerala, India
e-mail: safna_p180029ph@nitc.ac.in

R. A. Maurya
e-mail: ramajor@nitc.ac.in

G. K. Rajanikant and P. Pré (eds.), *Perspectives on Global Transformation*, Lecture Notes in Electrical Engineering 1368, https://doi.org/10.1007/978-981-96-6707-9_8

mode or first harmonic $n = 1$, the loop oscillated with P_1 period and the nodes are seen at the footpoint of the loop. Similarly, for second harmonic $n = 2$, the loop has two periods P_1 and P_2 and the node also seen at the loop top and two sides of the loop oscillates in anti-phase to each other and so on. Many researchers, including Ruderman, Verwichte, Andries and Doorsselaere [5, 10–12] studied the applications of harmonics with different models. In this way, the observations and analyses of higher harmonics provide a different seismological implication mainly in the aspect of magnetic field variation and density stratification along the coronal loop, loop curvature, flux tube expansion, etc.

In addition to studying the decaying oscillations in the fundamental mode, decayless cases were also investigated [13]. Mostly observed transverse coronal loop oscillations (TLOs) are fastly damped within a few periods, mainly due to damping mechanisms like resonant absorption or mode coupling [14]. These analyses contribute to understanding the behavior and dynamics of coronal loops during the flare eruptions, helps to determine the density, magnetic field strength, temperature, etc., of the coronal plasma and shedding light on the complex interplay between magnetic fields and plasma dynamics in the solar atmosphere.

This paper deals with observations of harmonics in coronal loop oscillations. The oscillatory information is utilized to deduce the Alfv'en speed, and the magnetic field strength inside the oscillating loop. Section 2 includes the data used for the study. Analysis and results are discussed in Sect. 3, and Sect. 4 summarizes the results and conclusions.

2 Observational Data

We use observations from SDO/AIA for the analysis. The AIA has two ultraviolet (UV) and seven extreme ultraviolet (EUV) bandpasses. The EUV provides seven continuous full-disk images of the Sun with a temporal cadence of 12 s and a pixel resolution of $0''.6$. One of them is 304 Å, which emits from He II. The others are EUV wavelengths with iron emission bands: 171 Å, 131 Å, 94 Å, 193 Å, 211 Å and 335 Å.

3 Analysis and Results

The active region NOAA 12860 was situated at a latitude of 28° south and a longitude of 10° west. It was a disk AR with no neighborhood strong field regions. From GOES soft X-ray flux, we observe an M4.7 class flare that started on 05:39 UT, peaking at 06:11 UT, and ending has at 06:23 UT. This flare occurs at a position of S27W01 within the AR. The AR coronal loop (see dotted blue curve in the left panel of Fig. 1) is further used for the oscillation studies. This study is carried out from 'P' to 'Q' direction. Thus, we take the event duration from 05:00 UT to 07:00 UT on August 28, 2021.

For studying the different mode of the coronal loop oscillations, initially, we chose the loop L_1 from the AIA 171 Å images which is easily distinguishable among the loop bundle (see left panel of Fig. 1). Then, we placed a 'PQ' segment across the loop in an arbitrary perpendicular direction (see white solid line in left panel of the Fig. 1) to check the clear oscillatory patterns along that direction. Then, a time-space map created by tracking loop's intensity with respect to time along that 'PQ'. Change the 'PQ' direction until obtain an oscillatory pattern with enough number of oscillation cycles.

We extracted the time series of displaced loop positions from the time-space intensity map by analyzing the intensity along the 'PQ'. Then repeat this methods more than five times to get accurate loop positions. Then, the mean and standard deviation taken as the average loop position (see white crosses in right panel of the Fig. 1 and left panel of Fig. 2) and error in the estimation respectively. For more details about the identification and estimation of coronal loop positions, refer researchers such as Jain and safna Banu [15–17] who had done the similar procedures.

From the time-space intensity map in the right panel of the Fig. 1, the white crosses represented the mean position of the loop or the wave patterns which are decaying with more than one component of frequency as a function of the time. This implies that, the observed coronal loop oscillated in higher harmonics with the decaying amplitude. In order to verify the multiple mode of oscillations in the coronal loop, we used the Fourier spectral analysis of the time series.

From Fig. 2, the right panel shows the computed Fourier Power Spectra (FPS) of the time series of L_1 in the left panel. The dotted vertical lines in the right panel are the three peak periods obtained from the FPS analysis. The FPS confirms that

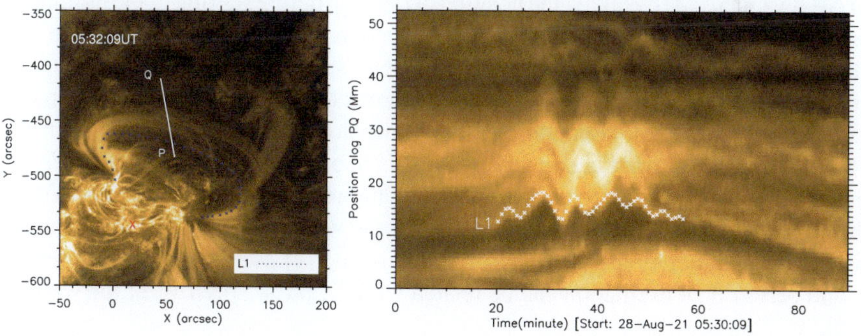

Fig. 1 Coronal loops traced in SDO/AIA. The left panel represents AIA 171 Å intensity images of the oscillation event with projected coronal loop coordinates marked with blue dotted curves which taken before the start of the oscillation. The white solid line 'PQ' mark an arbitrary slit position across the loop, which is further used to create time-space map as shown in the right panel. The white crosses represent in the right panel are the mean positions of the oscillated coronal loop L_1

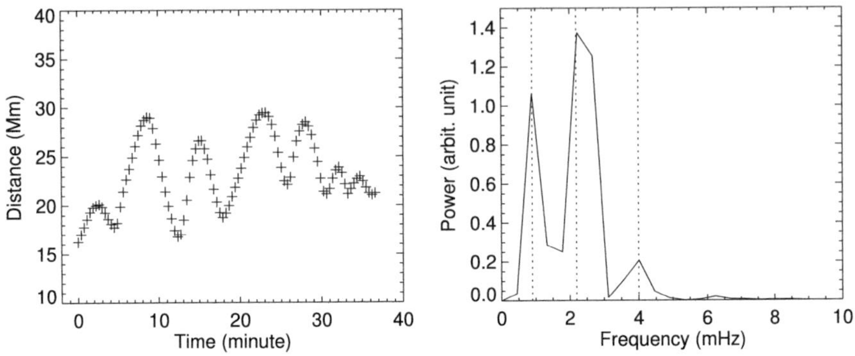

Fig. 2 Left panel crosses present the mean loop positions taken from the time-space map (crosses in the right panel of Fig. 1) along 'PQ' and the evaluated Fourier Power Spectra (FPS) of the time series are shown in Right panel

Table 1 The period P, kink speed C_k, Alfvén speed V_{A0}, and the magnetic field strength B in the coronal loops along the 'PQ' direction for the first ($n = 1$), second ($n = 2$) and third ($n = 3$) harmonics

Loop	Period, P (min)			Length L (mm)	C_k (km s^{-1})			V_{A0} (km s^{-1})			B (G)
	1	2	3		1	2	3	1	2	3	1
L_1	18.5	7.6	4.2	172	400	754	1365	300	559	1012	11

L_1 is in the third mode of harmonic oscillation along this slit direction with periods $P_1 = 18.5$ min, $P_2 = 7.6$ min, and $P_3 = 4.2$ min (see Table 1).

To calculate the oscillated coronal loop length, we followed the method mentioned in Aschwanden [14] by taking the position of the loop before starting of the oscillation and its foot point locations. Repeat the procedure for five times. The mean and standard deviation values are taken as the loop position and error in the calculation (for references see papers [15–17]). Thus, the projected coronal loop length estimated as $L = 172$ Mm. The evaluation of three dimensional geometry and length of the coronal loop can be done accurately with the help of solar stereoscopy [18]. We did not adopt this method due to the lack of observational data. Further, one can estimate the kink speed C_k, Alfvén speed V_{A0}, and the magnetic field strength B by using the oscillation and loop properties. Thus, for an nth mode of oscillation, the loop length L and period P of oscillation can be related with the phase speed V_n of the wave as [19],

$$V_n = \frac{2L}{nP}. \tag{1}$$

For a fundamental mode of oscillation ($n = 1$), the magnetic field strength inside of a coronal loop can be deduced (for more details refer the papers [2, 16, 20]) as,

$$B = V_{A0}\sqrt{\mu_0 \mu_c m_p n_e}, \tag{2}$$

where, m_p is the proton mass and $\mu_c = 1.27$ is the mean molecular weight in the corona. Thus, the estimated coronal loop parameters are listed in Table 1 along the arbitrary 'PQ' direction. Thus, coronal seismology gives an average value of the magnetic field inside an oscillating coronal loop [2]. But, the density and magnetic field are vary along the loop [4], which can be calculated with another method like extrapolating magnetic field in the lower layers into the solar corona [21, 22]. Sometimes, this method faces failures [23].

4 Summary and Conclusions

We conduct this experiment to achieve an understanding of how magnetic structures like coronal loops behave as an oscillator or waveguide while magnetohydrodynamic (MHD) waves especially the transverse kink waves are generated within it due to explosive events like a solar flare. We studied the parameters such as periods, amplitude, phase, mode, and damping time associated with the oscillations. These oscillatory parameters are combined with the proposed theoretical models, this method is called coronal seismology, to deduce coronal plasma parameters including the plasma density, magnetic field strength, and the temperature distribution within the coronal loops.

The analysed coronal loop nestled within the dynamic active region, AR NOAA 12680, prominently displaying a sigmoidal configuration on the sun's surface. This particular region exhibited hallmark features characteristic of sigmoidal formations, including eruptions, coronal wave propagation, and the occurrence of notable solar flares such as the GOES C7.0 and M4.7 class flares, the latter accompanied by a Coronal Mass Ejection (CME). Notably, one of these events acted as a predecessor for the subsequent observation of harmonic oscillations. Our initial investigative focus was directed towards identifying the mode of oscillation, succeeded by a meticulous evaluation of oscillatory parameters along a predefined slit direction. Specifically, we delved into the analysis of coronal loop oscillations driven by a solar flare graded at M4.7 within the aforementioned active region. Our scrutiny uncovered the presence of harmonic oscillations within a distinct coronal loop structure, substantiated by comprehensive Fourier spectral analysis, which delineated three discernible periods of oscillation: 18.5 minutes, 7.6 minutes, and 4.2 minutes, respectively. Furthermore, our precise measurements of the oscillating loop's length, estimated at 172 Mm, enabled the derivation of magnetic field strength estimated as 11 gauss (G) inside the coronal loop.

In addition to these findings, the observations and analysis of harmonics in coronal loops give another implementation to coronal seismology, especially, the ratio of the period of oscillations states how the plasma density, magnetic field, and temperature are distributed in the coronal loops, loop curvature, etc., can also be estimated. It has a wide range of acceptance nowadays, particularly in the field of the coronal heating problem—a question about how the solar surface is hotter than the solar atmosphere, that is, these MHD waves can transfer energy to heat the coronal plasma. Thus, in summary, the study of MHD waves provides insight into the solar atmospheric dynamics and the coronal heating mechanism.

Acknowledgements This work uses the observational data obtained from the AIA/SDO, EUVI/STEREO-A and LASCO/SOHO. SOHO is project of international collaboration between ESA and NASA. The integrated X-ray flux data were obtained from GOES operated by National Oceanic and Atmospheric Administration, USA. One of the authors, RAM, acknowledges support from the ISRO RESPOND project.

References

1. Aschwanden MJ, Fletcher L, Schrijver CJ, Alexander D (1999) Coronal loop oscillations observed with the transition region and coronal explorer. Astrophys J 520(2):880–894
2. Nakariakov VM, Ofman L, DeLuca EE, Roberts B, Davila JM (1999) TRACE observation of damped coronal loop oscillations: implications for coronal heating. Science 285(5429):862–864
3. Zimovets IV, Nakariakov VM (2015) Excitation of kink oscillations of coronal loops: statistical study. Astron Astrophys 577:A4
4. Aschwanden MJ, Schrijver CJ (2011) Coronal loop oscillations observed with atmospheric imaging assembly-kink mode with cross-sectional and density oscillations. Astrophys J 736(2):102
5. Verwichte E, Nakariakov VM, Ofman L, Deluca EE (2004) Characteristics of transverse oscillations in a coronal loop arcade. Solar Phys 223(1–2):77–94
6. Andries J, Goossens M, Hollweg JV, Arregui I, Doorsselaere TV (2005) Coronal loop oscillations. Astron Astrophys 430(3):1109–1118
7. Andries J, Doorsselaere TV, Roberts B, Verth G, Verwichte E, Erdélyi R (2009) Coronal seismology by means of kink oscillation overtones. Space Sci Rev 149(1–4):3–29
8. Moortel ID, Brady CS (2007) Observation of higher harmonic coronal loop oscillations. Astrophys J 664(2):1210–1213
9. Li H, Liu Y, Tam KV (2017) Fundamental and harmonic oscillations in neighboring coronal loops. Astrophys J 842(2):99
10. Ruderman MS (2003) The resonant damping of oscillations of coronal loops with elliptic cross-sections. Astron Astrophys 409(1):287–297
11. Andries J, Arregui I, Goossens M (2005) Determination of the coronal density stratification from the observation of harmonic coronal loop oscillations. Astrophys J 624(1):L57–L60
12. Doorsselaere TV, Nakariakov VM, Verwichte E (2007) Coronal loop seismology using multiple transverse loop oscillation harmonics. Astron Astrophys 473(3):959–966
13. Nisticò G, Nakariakov VM, Verwichte E (2013) Decaying and decayless transverse oscillations of a coronal loop. Astron Astrophys 552:A57
14. Aschwanden MJ, Pontieu BD, Schrijver CJ, Title AM (2002) Transverse oscillations in coronal loops observed with trace II. Measurements of geometric and physical parameters. Solar Phys 206(11):99–132. Provided by the SAO/NASA Astrophysics Data System
15. Jain R, Maurya RA, Hindman BW (2015) Fundamental-mode oscillations of two coronal loops within a solar magnetic arcade. Astrophys J 804(1):L19
16. Banu KS, Maurya RA, Jacob PTJ (2022) Transverse oscillation of coronal loops induced by eruptions of a magnetic flux tube and a plasmoid. Solar Phys 297(10)
17. Safna Banu K, Maurya RA (2024) Flare-induced transverse oscillations of coronal loops and propagating euv waves, vol 14 [Online]. Available: #www.tnsroindia.org.inIJONS#
18. Aschwanden MJ, Wuelser J-P, Nitta NV, Lemen JR, DeRosa ML, Malanushenko A (2012) First three dimensional reconstruction of coronal loops with the stereo a+b spacecraft. IV. Magnetic modeling with twisted force-free fields. Astrophys J 756(2):124

19. Nakariakov VM, Ofman L (2001) Determination of the coronal magnetic field by coronal loop oscillations. Astron Astrophys 372(3):L53–L56
20. Roberts B, Edwin PM, Benz AO (1984) On coronal oscillations. Astrophys J 279:857
21. Schatten KH, Wilcox JM, Ness NF (1969) A model of interplanetary and coronal magnetic fields. Solar Phys 6(3):442–455
22. Wiegelmann T (2004) Optimization code with weighting function for the reconstruction of coronal magnetic fields. Solar Phys 219(1):87–108
23. Aschwanden MJ, Wülser J-P, Nitta N, Lemen J (2012) Solar stereoscopy with STEREO/EUVI a and b spacecraft from small (6 degree) to large (170 degree) spacecraft separation angles. Solar Phys

Quasi Periodic Oscillation in a Coronal Mass Ejection Due to Shock Wave

Sachin Rajkapoor Kanaujiya, Ram Ajor Maurya, and P. T. Jain Jacob

Abstract Quasi-periodic pulsations (QPPs) in solar and stellar flares pose a persistent puzzle in solar physics due to their unclear origins. This paper investigates the potential connection between coronal mass ejections (CMEs) and the generation of QPP, particularly focusing on observations of the K-corona using white-light. Notably, a post-CME shock wave emerges as a candidate mechanism driving QPP, as evidenced by distinctive features in the observed light curve. Employing the global wavelet transform technique, we identify an eight-minute oscillation associated with the shock wave, hinting at a potential link between magnetoacoustic waves in the corona and the observed QPP phenomena. The study contributes to clarifying the origins of QPP by identifying the post-CME shock wave as a potential driver of this phenomenon.

Keywords Quasi-periodic pulsation · Coronal mass ejection · Magnetohydrodynamic shock · Solar flares · Stellar flares

1 Introduction

Solar flares are abrupt release of magnetic field energy accumulated in the active region corona as a result of magnetic reconnection [1]. CMEs are another example of explosive events that frequently cause massive amounts of coronal plasma to be ejected into interplanetary space at up to speed of 3000 km/s [2]. Many intermittent

S. R. Kanaujiya (✉) · R. A. Maurya · P. T. Jain Jacob
National Institute of Technology Calicut, Kozhikode, Kerala, India
e-mail: sachin_p220261ph@nitc.ac.in

R. A. Maurya
e-mail: ramajor@nitc.ac.in

P. T. Jain Jacob
e-mail: jain_p180130ph@nitc.ac.in

G. K. Rajanikant and P. Pré (eds.), *Perspectives on Global Transformation*, Lecture Notes in Electrical Engineering 1368, https://doi.org/10.1007/978-981-96-6707-9_9

and oscillatory features appear during flares and CMEs and are important diagnostic markers for understanding plasma dynamics and properties during magnetic reconnection and such eruption events.

QPPs are the temporal oscillations in the light curve of the solar and stellar flares.These pulsations manifest as periodic fluctuations in intensity or emission characteristics across multiple wavelengths, including X-ray [3, 4] , ultraviolet [5], optical [6], microwave [7], and radio bands [8]. QPPs has been seen in all phase of solar flares, i.e., start, peak and in decay phase. QPPs has also been seen sometime related to the magnetohydrodynamic (MHD) oscillations of magnetic structure such as coronal loops [9] and sometimes following the magnetic reconnections [9]. Interplanetary shocks are largely produced by CMEs [10]. Nevertheless, the exact source of coronal shockwaves is still a matter of debate and requires further investigation. There have been two primary physical interpretations put forth: a blast wave set out by a flare's energetic or as an alternative, a CME-induced shock powered by a pressure pulse.

In this paper, we have analysed coronal H-alpha intensity images associated with a CME and found a temporal oscillatory pattern in the intensity variation of CME associated with the shock wave. In Sect. 2 we have discussed the observational data and then in Sect. 3 we have shown the result and analysis of CME data, finally in the Sect. 4 we have given the conclusion and future work regarding this work.

2 Observational Data

The data used in this paper has been taken from the Ground-based observatory telescope located in Hawaii named Mauna Loa Solar Observatory. The Mauna Loa K-Coronagraph (K-Cor) [11] is a new instrument designed to study solar corona and coronal mass ejection (CME) events. K-Cor's field of view ranges from 1.05 to 3 solar radii, allowing us to monitor the lower and middle corona where coronal mass ejections emerge and develop. It records the polarization brightness (pB) in the passbands of 720–750 nm.

Data used in the analysis is the level-2 fits data of size (1024,1024) containing a coronal polarization brightness image. The images display calibrated coronal polarization brightness, expressed in units of B/B_{sun}, where B_{sun} denotes the brightness of the solar disk itself. The spatial and temporal resolution of the images are 11.3 arcseconds (5.643 arcsec/pix) and 15 s respectively.

This brightness arises from photospheric photons undergoing Thomson scattering by coronal electrons. Consequently, the brightness intensity reflects the electron density along the observer's line of sight to the corona. Typically falling between 10^{-6} and 10^{-9} B/B_{sun} within the K-Cor field of view (ranging from 1.05 to 3 solar radii), the observed pB values are averaged over 15 s to achieve a sufficient signal-to-noise ratio and ensure robust measurements.

3 Analysis and Results

We have considered a perpendicular slit across the coronal mass ejection shock wave to see how, with time, CME is moving across the slit AB, as we can see in Fig. 1. The CME has bright front, a dark cavity and a bright compact core with structured prominence in the northeast limb at approximately 50 ° position angle (PA) from 17:12 to 19:04 UT. To make the perpendicular slit along the shock wave, a circle has been drawn by considering the sun center in the fits image file. A straight line has been made to pass through the center of the parabolic shock wave and sun, and at the edge of the parabolic shock, a perpendicular line to the straight line has been made by touching the edge of the shock.

Figure 2, shows a space-time map along the slit AB. We can clearly see the shock front and CME features during 18:00–18:30 UT and 18:30–19:00 UT, respectively. To study the QPP in CME, we extracted the intensity slit across the CME position from the space time map. The intensity plot of the shock wave has been fitted with the mean of the plot and after subtracting the mean trend we have found a quasi-periodic oscillation in coronal mass ejection due to the shock wave, refer to Fig. 3a.

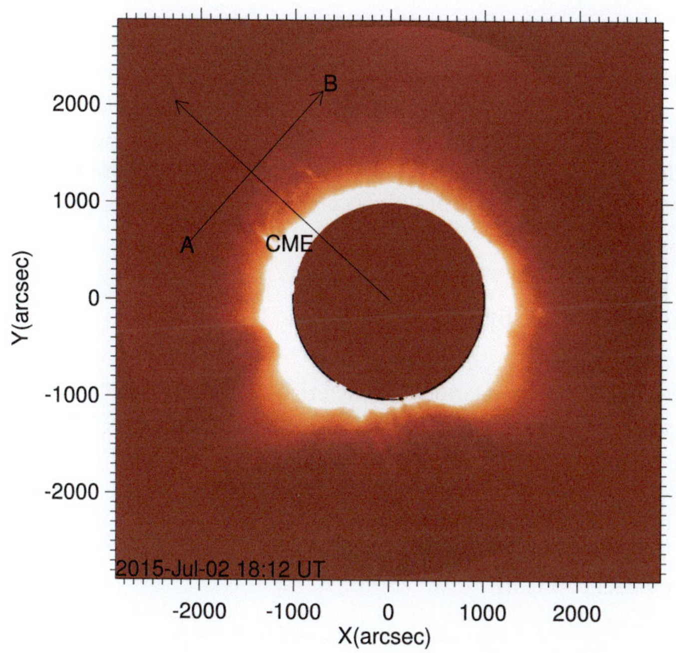

Fig. 1 H-α intensity image of the solar K-corona. The line segment AB, perpendicular to the radial direction from the sun-center, represents the slit along which space-time maps are constructed

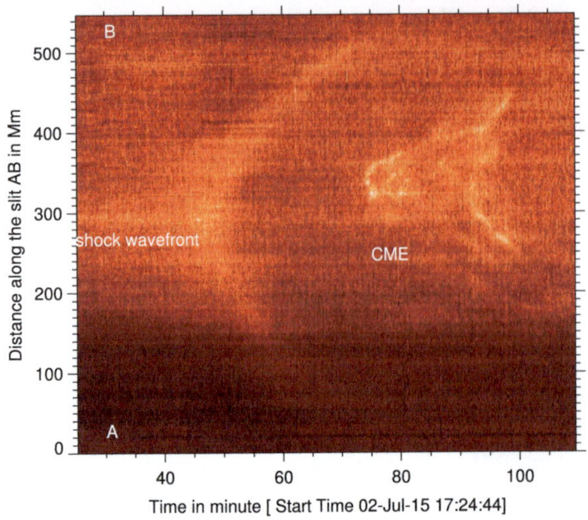

Fig. 2 The space-time map of Hα intensity along the perpendicular slit AB, as shown in Fig. 1, depicting the positions of the shock and the CME

Now to analyze the oscillation, the global wavelet transform has been used to determine its period and the significance level. We found large power in the oscillation, Fig. 3b–d. The analysis identified a notable quasi-periodic oscillation with a period of 8 min in the CME event through the application of wavelet transform methods. This oscillation is particularly significant, with a confidence level exceeding 95%, and it remains outside the cone of influence.

4 Summary and Conclusions

This study clarifies the mysterious characteristics of QPPs, which are detected in solar and stellar flares. The study explores the connection between CMEs and QPP formation by examining data from the ground-based Mauna Loa Solar Observatory, with a special emphasis on the white-light wavelength of the K-corona. Similar to previous studies that have detected long-period pulsations in white light observations ([6]), our analysis has also uncovered an 8-minute oscillation in the white light coronagraph data of a CME.

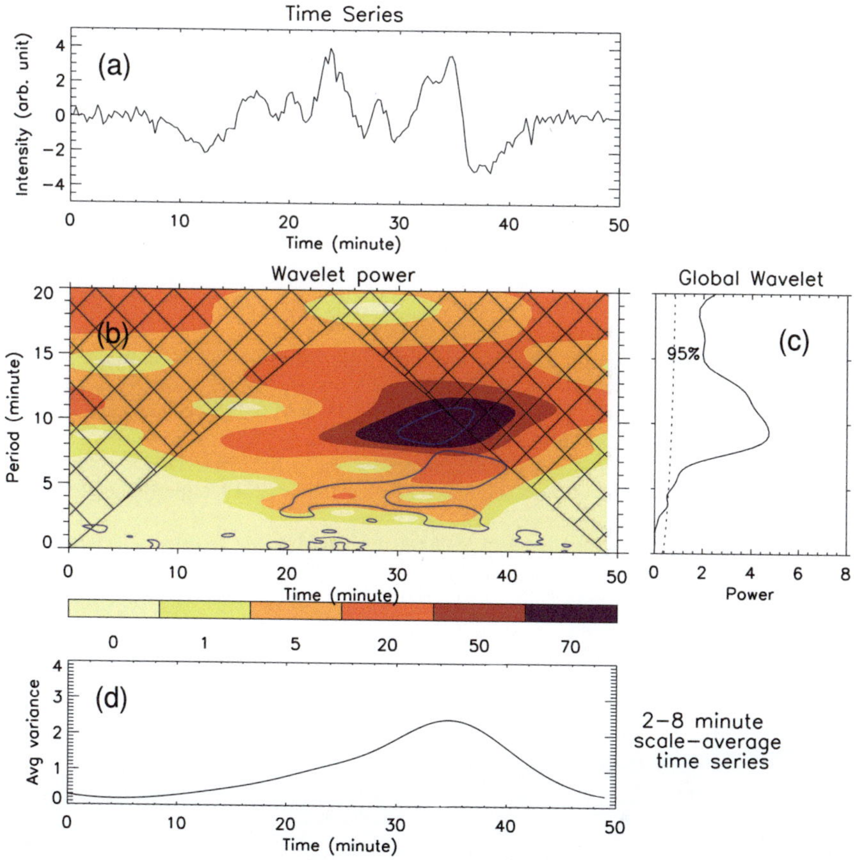

Fig. 3 **a** Light curve of the CME event, **b** wavelet power and the cone of influence, **c** global wavelet transform with a significance of oscillation above 95%, and **d** average power spectra of the oscillation as a function of time

The analysis of temperature distributions in the corona will be the main focus of future research since it can reveal information about the underlying physical processes. In addition, analyzing wave modes to pinpoint particular oscillation types and researching the dynamics of the magnetic field will be necessary to differentiate between these mechanisms. To further improve our understanding of QPP formation and its relationship to CME-related phenomena, numerical simulations and high-resolution observational data will be crucial.

Acknowledgements Courtesy of the Mauna Loa Solar Observatory, operated by the High Altitude Observatory, as part of the National Center for Atmospheric Research (NCAR). NCAR is supported by the National Science Foundation. One of the authors, RAM, acknowledges support from the ISRO RESPOND project.

References

1. Takahashi T, Qiu J, Shibata K (2017) Astrophys J 848(2):102. https://doi.org/10.3847/1538-4357/aa8f97
2. Illing RME, Hundhausen AJ (1986) J Geophy Res 91(A10):10951. https://doi.org/10.1029/JA091iA10p10951
3. Zimovets IV, Nechaeva AB, Sharykin IN, Nizamov BA (2022) Geomagn Aeron 62(4):356. https://doi.org/10.1134/S0016793222040181
4. Ning Z, Wang Y, Hong Z, Li D (2022) Solar Phys 297(1):2. https://doi.org/10.1007/s11207-021-01935-w
5. Su JT, Shen YD, Liu Y (2012) Astrophys J 754(1):43. https://doi.org/10.1088/0004-637X/754/1/43
6. Li D, Lu L, Ning Z, Feng L, Gan W, Li H (2020) Astrophys J 893(1):7. https://doi.org/10.3847/1538-4357/ab7cd1
7. Kou Y, Cheng X, Wang Y, Yu S, Chen B, Kontar EP, Ding M (2022) Nat Commun 13:7680. https://doi.org/10.1038/s41467-022-35377-0
8. Gotwols BL (1972) Solar Phys 25(1):232. https://doi.org/10.1007/BF00155759
9. Nakariakov VM, Melnikov VF (2009) Space Sci Rev 149(1–4):119. https://doi.org/10.1007/s11214-009-9536-3
10. Gopalswamy N, Yashiro S, Akiyama S (2006) In: Gopalswamy N, Bhattacharyya A (ed) Proceedings of the ILWS workshop, p 79
11. K-Cor Team (2013) Cosmo k-coronagraph (k-cor) white light polarization brightness images. 10.5065/D69G5JV8

Power and Area Efficient VLSI Algorithms for Auditory Compensation in Digital Hearing Aids

Ani Abraham, Manju Manuel, and P. G. Geo

Abstract Very Large Scale Integration (VLSI) algorithms play a crucial role in Semiconductor Technology. With the advancements in the field of VLSI technology, all kinds of electronic equipment have improved their performance in all aspects that span from the design basic to the reliability enhancements. In this paper, hardware efficient techniques are used for the realization of digital filter banks for auditory compensation. Auditory compensation is the heart of a digital hearing aid and filter banks are employed to split incoming audio signals into various frequency bands. To divide the audio spectrum, non uniform filter banks are preferred over uniform filter banks as they align more precisely with human ear's frequency resolution. Octave and fractional interpolated filter banks are used for creating non uniform filter banks. The key idea of this work is to replace the multipliers in these filter banks with more efficient multipliers which use VLSI algorithms like shift and add and vedic. The performance of these schemes are compared in terms of utilization and power and a remarkable improvement is achieved.

Keywords Digital hearing aids · Auditory compensation · Octave and fractional interpolated filter banks · IEEE 754 single precision floating point number · Vedic multiplier · Shift and add multiplier

---

Manju Manuel and P. G. Geo—These authors contributed equally to this work.

A. Abraham (✉)
Department of Electronics and Communication Engineering, Rajiv Gandhi Institute of Technology Kottayam, Affiliated to A P J Abdul Kalam Technological University, Kottayam, Kerala, India
e-mail: aniabraham@rit.ac.in

M. Manuel
Department of Electronics and Communication Engineering, Government Engineering College, Idukki, Affiliated to A P J Abdul Kalam Technological University, Kottayam, Kerala, India

P. G. Geo
Department of Electronics Engineering, Government Polytechnic College, Pala, Kottayam, Kerala, India

G. K. Rajanikant and P. Pré (eds.), *Perspectives on Global Transformation*, Lecture Notes in Electrical Engineering 1368, https://doi.org/10.1007/978-981-96-6707-9_10

1 Introduction

As per the latest update of World Health Organization, it is estimated that more than 5% of the population of the whole world, that is around 430 million people are suffering from various types of hearing losses and by 2050, this will increase to around 2.5 billion. And more that, there exists a huge gap between the requirement and availability of appropriate hearing aids [1]. This threatening fact indicates the need for the availability of hearing aids that are superior in performance and, at the same time, affordable to everyone. So the development of efficient and cost effective hearing aids are of prime importance. Digital hearing aids have various sections analog to digital converter and digital to analog converter, auditory compensation section, feedback cancellation, noise cancellation etc. [2]. Among these sections, auditory compensation section is known as the heart of the hearing aid. Lot of works have been going on in optimizing the performance of this section. Studies have shown that ANSI S1.11 1/3 octave filter banks are best suited for processing audio spectrum of hearing aid at the expense of high complexity [3]. Non uniform digital linear phase FIR filter banks give good results when used in 8 band, 16 band or 17 band channel applications [4–6]. The Short-Time Fourier Transform (STFT) is a powerful technique used in digital hearing aids for auditory compensation. It involves analyzing various segments of a signal to determine how its frequencies change over time. This is particularly useful in hearing aids, where it can help to amplify only the frequencies that a person with hearing loss has trouble in hearing [7].

Most of the auditory compensation techniques utilize different types of filter banks which are made up of multipliers, adders and delay elements. It is possible to improve the efficiency of the hardware by incorporating VLSI algorithms instead of conventional binary adders and multipliers. Multipliers using Vedic Algorithm are very fast and efficient and this algorithm results in a reduction of area and power [8].

2 Digital Hearing Aids System An Overview

A digital hearing aid is a small electronics device that amplifies the weak sound signal. The purpose of this gadget is to compensate for the impairment in hearing and this is worn either inside the ear or behind the ear. Digital hearing aids use varied and customised signals to produce natural-sounding speech and audio that is enhanced with depth and diversity. This is in contrast to analog hearing aids that use continuous and uniform sound signals. These intelligent gadgets may be tailored to meet unique hearing requirements, adapt on their own to various listening environments, and even establish wireless connections with other Bluetooth devices. Various sections of a digital hearing aid are shown in the Fig. 1. As shown in the figure, the analog signal received from the microphone is converted to a high quality digital signal using an analog to digital converter (D/A converter) [9]. These digital signals or binary codes are fed to the auditory compensation section. This section compensate for the loss

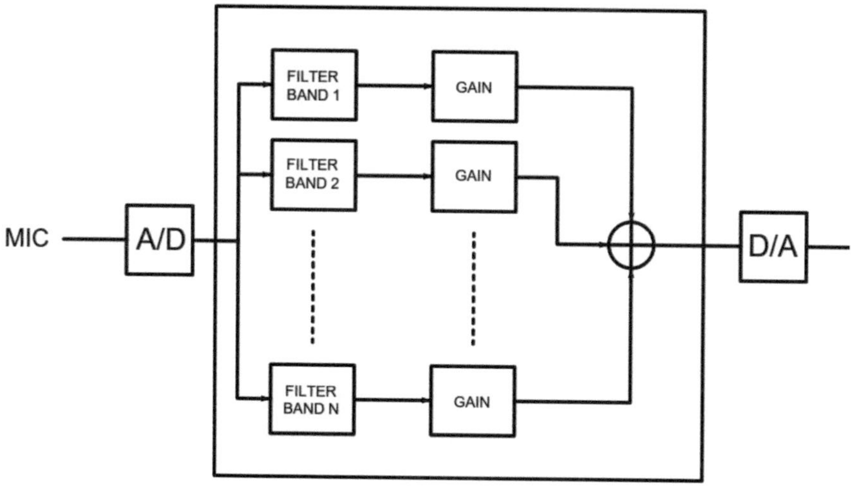

Fig. 1 Digital hearing aid—block diagram

in the hearing of the patient. The received audio signals are amplified based on the audiogram of the patient.

An audiogram is a graphical chart that visually represents the results of a hearing test. This chart represents frequency (pitch) ranging from 125 to 8 KHz in X axis and measures intensity (loudness) in dB in Y axis (ranges from -10 to 120 dB). A person with a normal hearing can hear quiet sounds of less than 20 dB, while 20–40 dB is classified under mild hearing loss, 41–70 dB is moderate hearing loss, 71–95 dB severe hearing loss and above 95 dB is very severe which is classified under profound hearing loss. Hearing threshold level of right ear is represented using 'O' and that of left ear is represented by 'X' (Fig. 2). The amplification of the received signals based on this audiogram is done with the help of a set of filter banks and gain adjustment blocks. Feedback cancellation and noise reduction are also done before finally converting the signal to an analog signal using a digital to analog converter (D/A converter).

3 Design of Filter Banks Digital Filter Banks

The concept of filter bank is to divide a complex signal in to simpler pieces called sub bands [10]. Each sub band carries a specific frequency range of the original signal. This enables the detailed examination of each sub band and processing accordingly. The process of sub band creation is done through multirate signal processing. The key idea behind multirate signal processing is to process signals at different sampling frequencies. Three different processes are involved in this, decimation, interpolation and resampling these frequencies. Decimation refers to the process of reducing the

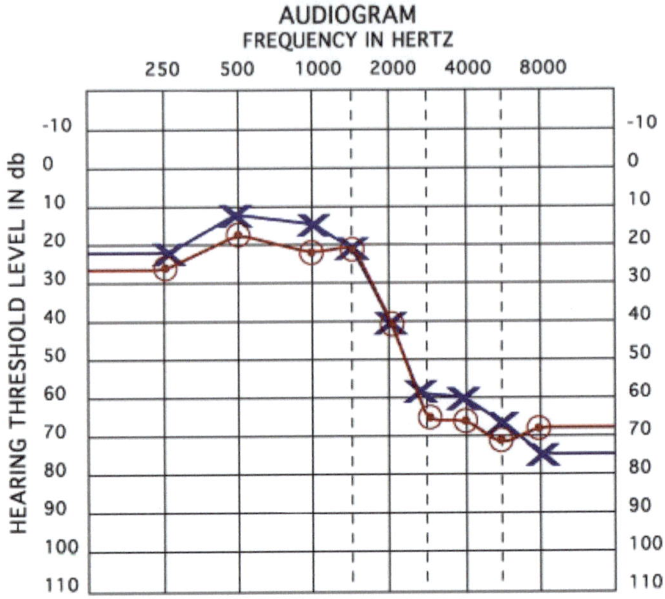

Fig. 2 Audiogram

signal's sampling rate. A positive integer M is used to denote decimation factor. When the process of down sampling the signal is done, all other samples other than Mth sample are ignored. The frequency spectrum will be expanded by M. Anti aliasing filters are used before decimation to band limit the signals. The reverse process of the decimation is called interpolation. Here up sampling is done which expands the sampling rate of the signal. Up sampling is also known as interpolation and denoted by letter L. In certain cases we need to change the sampling rate by a fractional number say L/M, otherwise it may cause aliasing. Such type of sampling is known as fractional sampling. So to summarise, three types of multirate filters: decimation filters, interpolation filters, and fractional decimation filters. The following equations summarize these three.

The following equation defines the M fold decimation filter

$$y(n) = \sum_{k=-\infty}^{\infty} x(k)h(nM - k), \tag{1}$$

The L fold interpolation filter is given below.

$$y(n) = \sum_{k=-\infty}^{\infty} x(k)h(n - kL), \tag{2}$$

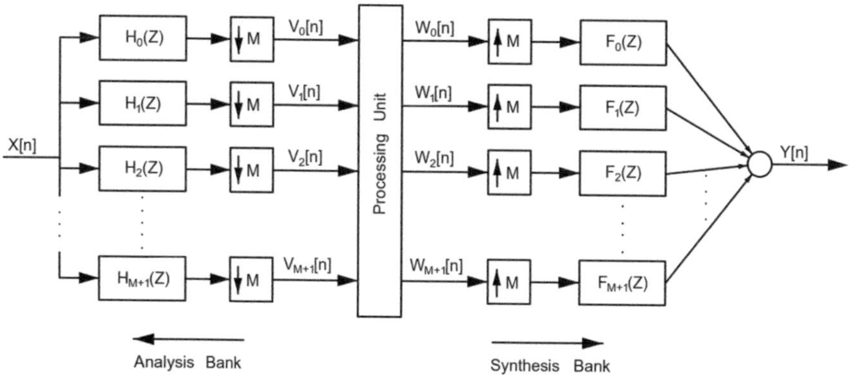

Fig. 3 M band digital filter bank

The M/L fold decimation filter is given below.

$$y(n) = \sum_{k=-\infty}^{\infty} x(k)h(nM - kL), \tag{3}$$

A group of digital filters is called a digital filter bank. Their input and output are identical. On the input side they have analysis banks and on the output side, they have synthesis filters. Analysis bank consists of M filters $H_k(z)$ which splits the input signal x(n) in to M sub band signals. Similarly synthesis bank includes $F_k(z)$ filters to reconstruct the output. Figure 3 shows a M band filter bank. In Digital hearing aids, the frequency spectrum we are concentrating is from the 125 Hz to 8kHz. This range is targeted to ensure that the most critical sounds for everyday listening are amplified, allowing users to communicate more effectively and perceive sounds more naturally.

4 Three Region Method for Auditory Compensation Section

A three region method with auto-reconfigurabilty is selected for the design of prototype filter [11]. Three region method divides the entire band in to three equal regions, and the bandwidth of each region is $\Pi/3$. Up to 2.67 kHz frequency band is included by region 1, while from 2.67 to 5.34 kHz by region 2 and 5.34–8 kHz is in the third region. A prototype filter which is a linear phase FIR filter $H_l(z)$ is designed to cover region 1, and a high pass filter $H_h(z)$ is created from this to cover region 3. These two filters are used to produce the mid-band, $H_m(z)$. Various sub bands for these regions are created from the prototype filter by decimation, octave interpolation and fractional interpolation. Octave interpolation is generated by selecting L= 2^k.

For sub band generation, four schemes are adopted, where in scheme 1, only three bands, with band with $\Pi/3$ for each band. Scheme 2 is implemented by selecting k = 1 in octave interpolation. Bandwidth of each band is $\Pi/6$, resulting in six uniform bands. Schemes 3 and 4 are realized by selecting K = 2 and K=3 respectively resulting 9 band non uniform filter banks in scheme 3 and 17 band non uniform filter banks in scheme 4. The band width ranges from $\Pi/12$ to $\Pi/24$.

To select the optimum scheme is based the particular audiogram which is under processing, that in turn based on the slope of the audiogram in that particular region. When the audiogram is flat in the regions, lower schemes are opted. But audiogram response is steep in any particular region, higher schemes are selected.

5 Structure of the Auto Reconfigurable Three Region Method

The construction of the autoreconfigurable three region approach is depicted in Fig. 4. All filters shown are linear phase FIR filters. Each filter output consists of original and compliment components. 16 sub bands are generated using this structure through fractional and octave interpolation of the prototype filter. The positions of switches S_1, S_2, and S_3, decide which sub bands and thereby which scheme is selected. The switches are automatic switches operated based on the slope of the audiogram. All four schemes can be implemented using these sub bands. Hardware realization of these filters are done with symmetric filter coefficients, delay elements adders and multipliers.

6 Realization of the Reconfigurable Filter Bank Structure Using VLSI Algorithms

The delay units, adders, and multipliers make up the filter structure. The hardware efficiency of the structure can be increased by incorporating VLSI algorithms [12]. Here two types of multipliers, shift and adders and Vedic multipliers are used instead of conventional multipliers and the performance comparison in terms of power and speed are done. All units of this filter bank structure are designed with single precision floating point numbers.

6.1 IEEE754 Single Precision Floating Point Data Format

In the single precision floating point format, a floating radix point is utilised (IEEE754 single precision, sometimes referred to as FP32 (float32), a computer number for-

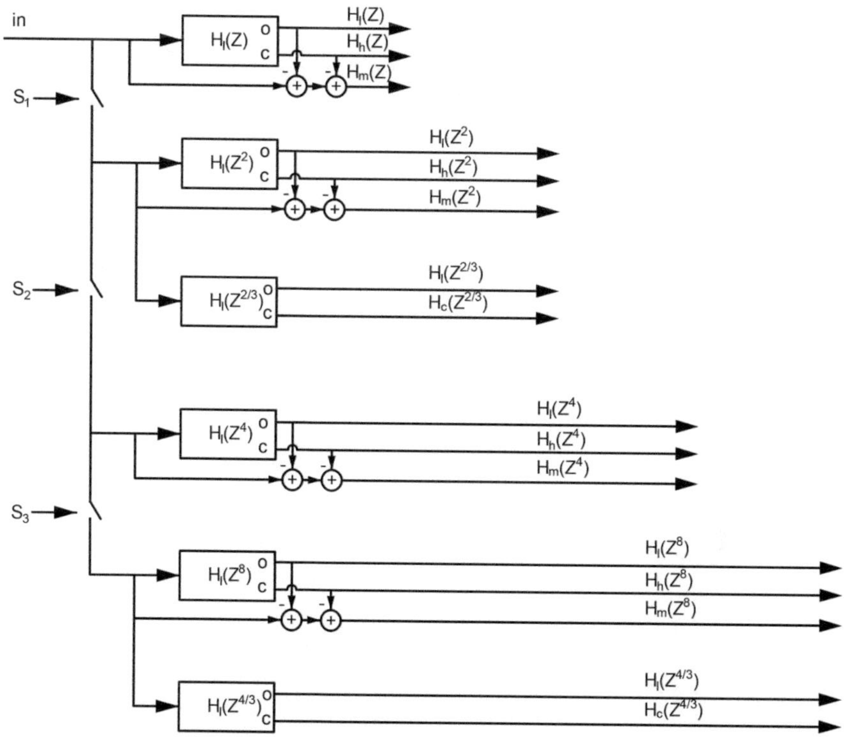

Fig. 4 Structure of the three region auto reconfigurable filter bank method

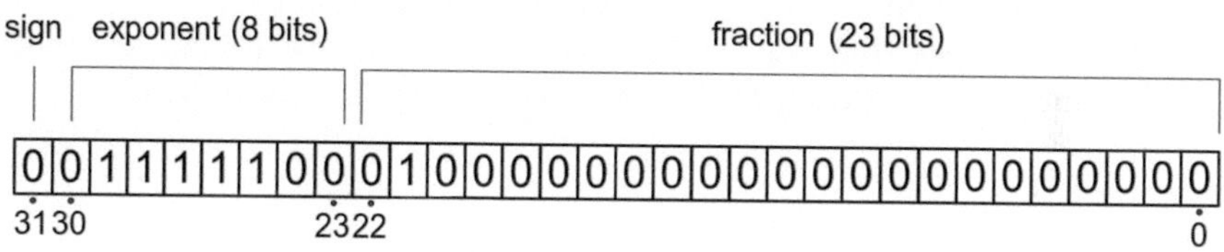

Fig. 5 IEEE 754 data format

mat that allows a wide dynamic range of numerical values to be expressed [13]. Figure 5 explains the data format of IEEE data format.

6.2 Delay Unit

A D flipflop is used as a delay unit. Two input terminals make up a D flip flop. One is given as clock input. D is the other data input. The complemented output is $\bar{Q}$, and the output is Q. Until the D input's state is altered and an active clock signal edge follows, the output stays constant. Before the clock transition, it stored data on its output and had no effect on the state. Put differently, the output is latched at a value of 0 or 1.

6.3 *Algorithm for Single Precision Floating Point Number Adder*

Figure 6 displays the basic block schematic for the single precision floating point addition. The sign bits of the numbers A1, A2, and A3 are denoted by S1, S2, and S3, respectively. E1, E2, and E3 are the exponent bits of the numbers A1, A2, and A3. M1, M2, and M3 are the mantissa bits of the numbers A1, A2, and A3.

A single precision floating point addition algorithm is presented here for the addition of two floating point numbers A1 and A2. Assume A3 is the sum. A3 = A1 + A2.

(1) E1 = E2, or the exponents of A1 and A2, must equal in order for the addition to occur.
(2) The greater of exponents E1 and E2 should be used to set exponent E3.
(3) Find the exponents E1 and E2 difference.
(4) Move the lower number's mantissa to the left based on the exponent difference. The exponents of A1 and A2 are discovered to be identical.
(5) Determine the mantissas' sum and difference using sign bits S1 and S2.
In case the signs of A1 and A2 are identical, add the mantissas.
In the event that A1 and A2's signs differ, subtract the mantissas.
(6) Normalise the resulting mantissa (1.M3 format) if required. The first exponent result must be adjusted in accordance with the mantissa normalisation.

6.4 *Algorithm for Multiplication Using Single Precision Floating Point Numbers*

Multiplication in IEEE 754 floating-point is easier than addition. The block diagram for the floating point multiplier unit is shown in Fig. 7. The sign bits of the numbers A1, A2, and A3 are denoted by S1, S2, and S3, respectively. E1, E2, and E3 are the exponent bits of the numbers A1, A2, and A3. Numbers A1, A2, and A3 have mantissa bits that are M1, M2, and M3. A single precision floating point multiplication algorithm for multiplying two floating point values, A1 and A2 is explained. Assume the product is A3. A3 = A1 * A2

(1) The first step is to check S1, the multiplicand's sign bit, and S2, the multiplier's sign bit, and XOR them. S3 is where the output is kept.

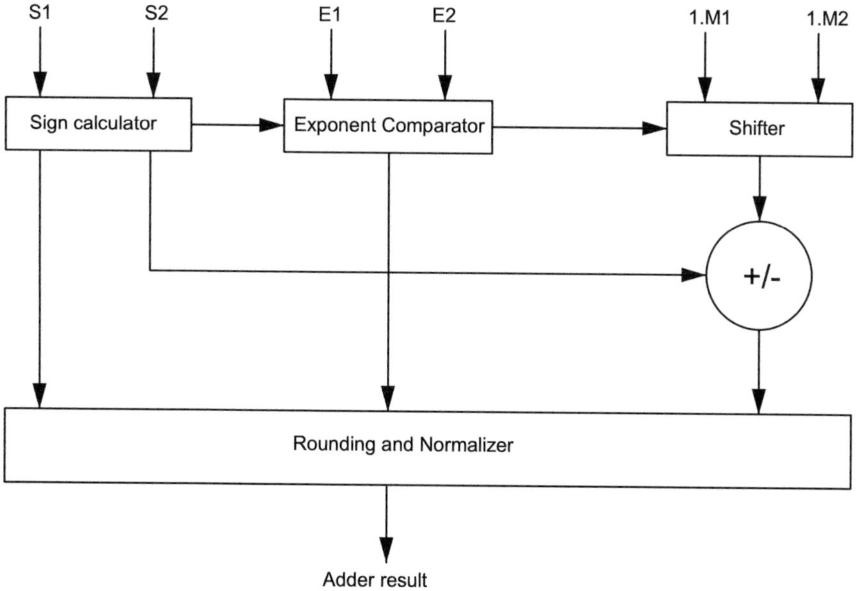

Fig. 6 Block schematic of addition using single precision floating point numbers

(2) After multiplying the mantissas of the A1 (M1) and A2 (M2), the result is stored as M3 (to make sure the result is not greater than 24 bits rounding/truncation is done). The result M3 is equal to M1 * M2.
(3) After adding the multiplicand exponent (E1) and multiplier exponent (E2), the bias value is subtracted from the total. The initial value of E3 is stored as the result of the subtraction.
(4) M3 can be normalised by moving to the left and decreasing the exponent or to the right and increasing the exponent.

6.5 Vedic Multiplier

The vedic multiplication algorithm in mathematics has been found in the Urdhva-Tiryakbhyam Sutra [14]. Because all partial products are generated simultaneously, the vedic multiplication approach is quick. The construction of a vedic multiplier is regular. Therefore, it is simple to raise the multiplier's bit size by widening the input and output data. Initially, a three by three block is implemented in order to prepare a twenty four x twenty four bit mantissa multiplier for a single precision floating point integer. The six by six block is constructed using the 3three by three block. A twelve by twelve block is designed using a six by six block. And at the end, a twenty four by twenty four block is used to create a twelve by twelve block. Vedic multipliers

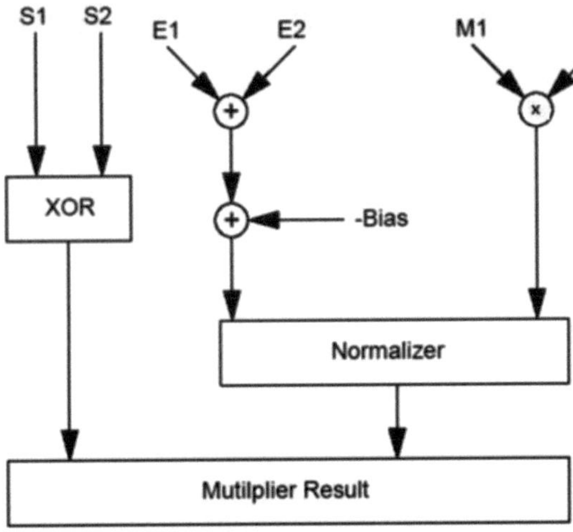

Fig. 7 Block diagram of single precision floating point multiplier

are faster than Array multiplier and Booth multiplier. As the number of bits in the operand increases, the delay is reduced in vedic multiplier. Figure 8 depicts a block diagram of a 24 × 24 bit vedic multiplier.

6.6 *Shift and Add Multiplier*

Shift and add is another efficient way of multiplication. To multiply two numbers, multiply the multiplicand by one multiplier digit, one at a time, from right to left. Then, move the intermediate product to the left of the previous results. The final product is the total of the intermediate products. The main advantages are simple, cost effective and accurate.

7 Hardware Implementation of the Structure

The structure is designed and coded using Verilog HDL and executed using Xilinx Vivado HLS 2020.1 on Xilinx Vertex 7 FPGA development board. Hardware utilization, and power consumption of different schemes are compared. Clock frequency selected is 16 Khz. The simulation result of the auditory compensation unit is shown in Fig. 9.

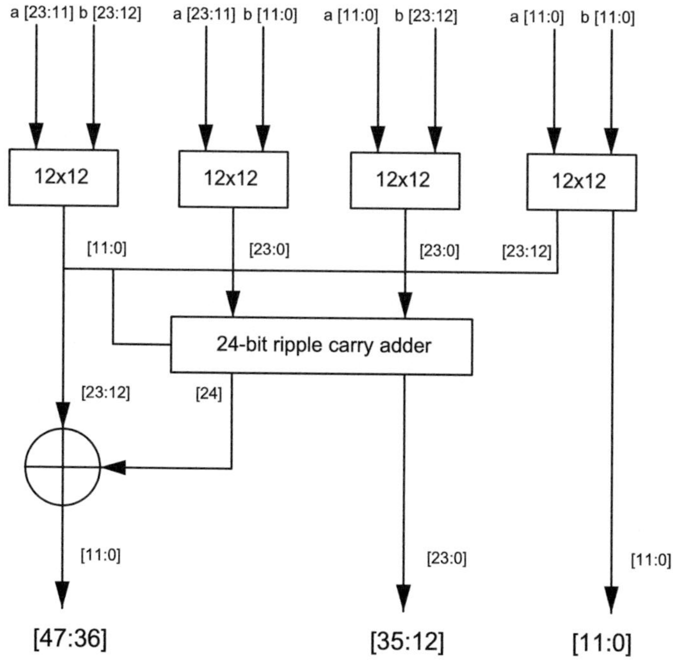

Fig. 8 Block diagram of a 24 × 24 bit vedic multiplie

7.1 Performance Comparison

After the simulation of the design, synthesis of the same is completed and synthesis report is generated. Hardware utilization and power consumption of conventional, shift and add and vedic multipliers are tabulated in Table 1. This table makes it clear that the auditory compensation section that used the vedic multiplier performs better than other structures of a similar kind. In vedic multipliers, the technology used for multiplication is parallel processing of partial products. This in turn will reduce the time taken for computation and therefore switching activity. Thus multipliers using vedic algorithm results in less power consumption. It is also seen that, the number of LUTs in shift and add method is more than conventional multiplier. But, conventional multipliers utilize two DSPs for the computation. Compared to method proposed in [11], data type used here is IEEE 754 single precision floating point number. By using IEEE 754 format, a wide range of real numbers with a standardized format can be represented. This makes floating-point arithmetic accurate and consistent across many computing platforms. Numerical computations are made more portable because to this standardisation.

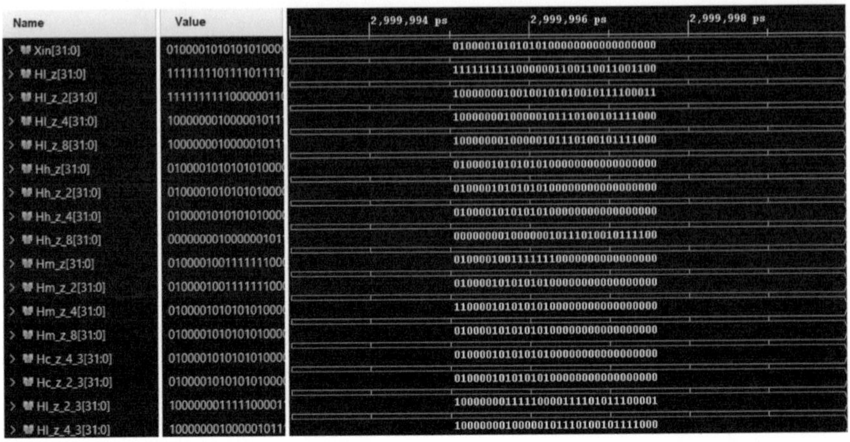

Fig. 9 Simulation results of the proposed system

Table 1 Synthesis report of the structure with different VLSI algorithms

Parameter	Shift and add multiplier	Vedic multiplier	Conventional multiplier
No. of slice LUTs	31273	27252	25863
Power consumption (Watt)	0.711	0.59	0.61
No. of DSPs used	Nil	Nil	2

8 Conclusion

Digital hearing aids with auto reconfigurabilty, i.e., the auditory compensation section based on the hearing impaired person's audiogram offers a very superior performance compared to the others. The hardware implementation of three region non uniform filter bank structure for digital hearing aid is proposed here. This structure is designed and implemented using efficient VLSI Algorithms. The data type used is 32 bit IEEE 754 floating point number for more accuracy and precision. The filter bank structure comprises of a number of multipliers, use of fast VLSI algorithms improves the overall efficiency. Savings in terms of area and power leads to superior performance of the device. Out of two VLSI algorithms used, vedic multiplier shows a remarkable superior performance. This type of designs will ultimately lead to superior performance and cost effective digital hearing aids.

References

1. World Health Organization Departmental News 2 March 2022
2. Kates JM (2008) Digital hearing aids. Plural Publishers
3. Liu CW, Chang KC , Chuang MH, Lin CH (2013) 10-ms 18-Band Quasi-ANSI S1.11 1/3-Octave filter bank for digital hearing aids. IEEE Trns Circ Syst I Regul Pap 60(3):638–649
4. Lian Y, Wei Y (2005) A computationally efficient nonuniform FIR digital filter bank for hearing aids. IEEE Trns Circ Syst I Regul Pap 52(12):2754–2762
5. Wei Y, Lian Y (2006) A 16-band nonuniform FIR digital filter bank for hearing aid. In: IEEE Biomedical circuits and systems conference. London, UK, pp 186–189
6. Devis T, Manuel M (2018) A 17-band non-uniform interpolated FIR filter bank for digital hearing aid. In: 2018 International conference on communication and signal processing (ICCSP). IEEE, pp 0452–0456
7. Krawczyk-Becker M, Gerkmann T (2014) STFT phase reconstruction in voiced speech for an improved single-channel speech enhancement. IEEE/ACM Trns Audio Speech Lang Process 22:1931–1940
8. Kivi Sona M, Somasundaram V (2020) Vedic multiplier implementation in VLSI. In: International conference on advances in material science and nanotechnology, vol 24, pp 2219–2230, part 4
9. Levitt H (2007) A historical perspective on digital hearing aids: how digital technology has changed modern hearing aids. Trends Amplif 11(1):7–24
10. Vaidyanathan PP (2006) Multirate systems and filter banks. Pearson Education India, New Delhi
11. Devis T, Manju M (2021) Hardware-efficient auto-reconfigurable hearing aids using 3-level octave interpolated filters for auditory compensation applications. Phys Eng Sci Med 44:785–798
12. VKR, ARS, NDR (2019) A comparative study on the performance of FPGA implementations of high-speed single-precision binary floating-point multipliers. In: International conference on smart systems and inventive technology (ICSSIT), pp 1041–1045
13. Brand M, Witterauf M, Bosio A, Teich J (2020) Anytime floating-point addition and multiplication-concepts and implementations. In: 2020 IEEE 31st international conference on application-specific systems, architectures and processors (ASAP), Manchester, UK, pp 157–164
14. Prabhu E, Mangalam H, Gokul PR (2019) A delay efficient Vedic multiplier. Proc Natl Acad Sci India Sect A Phys Sci 89:257–268

Technical and Scale Efficiency of Thermal Power Generation Companies in India: A DEA Approach

Sayan Chandran and Sunitha Sivaraman

Abstract India witnesses one of the fastest phases of economic growth, resulting in the fifth largest economy in the world. Further, the country surpassed China in terms of its population in 2023 and has the largest population in the world. Subsequent to policies resulting in a growth in manufacturing sector coupled with rapid urbanisation, large spending on infrastructure and housing, there has been a massive demand for electricity in India. Power generation companies play an important role in India's economy. However, there are lots of concerns in the power companies in India, including transmission and distribution losses, emissions of hazardous gas, and reliance on exported coal for production, which in turn makes the production costlier, resulting in weaker utilisation of resources. In this context, it is crucial to address how effectively the power companies in India utilise their resources. The study analyses the technical and scale efficiency of select private power companies in India during 2022–2023 financial year using Data Envelopment Analysis (DEA). The study has used an input-oriented model with multiple inputs, including number of employees, and capital expenditure, and outputs such as total power generated and total revenue with alternate models. The study also adds to the literature by also including undesirable output like sulphur dioxide emissions. The study finds that private companies are only 64–70% technically efficient during the period and the Reliance Power is the only company which is technically efficient across the alternate models. The scale efficiency estimates show that most of the companies are increasing returns to scale which calls for further possibility of expansion of production. The study further calls for research in the direction of more measures by considering the measures taken by the power plants to check emissions as input variables and to correlate with undesirable output as well as addressing the transmission and distribution of energy loss.

S. Chandran (✉)
Bachelors in Engineering Physics, National Institute of Technology, Calicut, Kozhikode, Kerala, India
e-mail: sayan_b200143ep@nitc.ac.in

S. Sivaraman
Department of Humanities, Arts and Social Sciences, National Institute of Technology Calicut, Kozhikode, Kerala, India
e-mail: sunita@nitc.ac.in

G. K. Rajanikant and P. Pré (eds.), *Perspectives on Global Transformation*, Lecture Notes in Electrical Engineering 1368, https://doi.org/10.1007/978-981-96-6707-9_11

Keywords Thermal power companies · Technical efficiency · Scale efficiency · Data envelopment analysis

1 Introduction

Power generation is considered as a major determinant of economic growth of a country. However, it may be noted that 40% of the global power generation is sourced from coal. In spite of rapid economic growth, the explosive rise in power generation sourced from coal and thermal sources have posed serious impacts on the economy in terms of depletion of foreign exchange reserves due to over reliance on imported coal as well as serious threats to the environment in terms of global warming resulting from the emissions.

India is the most populated country in the world, with a population of around 1.43 billion, i.e., around 17% of the world's population, and is the seventh largest country and the fifth largest economy in the world. India, the world's third largest energy consuming country following the United States (U.S) and China has seen its energy use doubling since 2000 (International Energy Agency (IEA), 2021). India has an installed capacity of 426.132 GW (Ministry of Power, 2024). Despite growing demand and rising capacity, about 80% of the demand for energy production in India is still met by solid biomass, coal, and oil (India Energy Outlook 2021, IEA). India's power sector is incredibly diverse, generating electricity from various sources. Conventional energy sources such as coal, oil, natural gas, nuclear power, and hydropower are used alongside unconventional sources like solar, wind, and domestic and agricultural waste. Coal is a significant source of energy in India, and around 75% of electricity is generated by coal. The electricity sector is the largest consumer of coal, using approximately 73% of the total coal consumption in India during the financial year 2021–22 (Ministry of Coal, Government of India, 2023). Moreover, India struggles with a puzzling situation of high coal imports despite possessing significant coal reserves within the country. While India possesses substantial coal reserves, demand often surpasses domestic production, so imports are necessary to meet the growing energy needs. This reliance on coal imports presents economic challenges and impedes sustainable development goals.

Additionally, India's transmission and distribution losses in the power sector remain considerably high. These losses occur during the transmission and distribution of electricity due to technical inefficiencies, theft, and other operational shortcomings (Ministry of Power, 2023). Addressing these losses is crucial to ensure a more efficient and reliable power supply across the country. Improving infrastructure, upgrading technologies, and implementing effective management strategies are essential to mitigate these challenges to achieve a more sustainable and efficient energy ecosystem in India. In this context, concerns related to optimal production, minimisation of transmission and distribution losses, reduction of emissions, and efficient allocation of funds for renewable energy based sources gather great prominence. The present study is a modest attempt to study the efficient allocation of resources of thermal private power companies in India.

The rest of the paper is organised as follows. Section 2 describes the background of the Indian energy sector, followed by a brief review of the literature in Sect. 3. The data, methodology, and model specification are detailed in Sect. 4, followed by a discussion of empirical estimates in Sect. 5. The last section concludes the paper.

2 Background of Energy Sector in India

India is the third largest producer and consumer of electricity in the world, with an installed capacity of 416.06 GW for electricity production in 2023. India produced almost 1,624.158 Billion Units (BU) of electricity in 2022–23, which includes 1206.21 BU of thermal energy (Central Electricity Regulation Authority (CERC), 2023).

Thermal is the major source of electricity generation in India, contributing almost 74% of the total electricity generation in 2022–23, followed by renewable energy sources (RES) (12.5%), hydro (10%), and nuclear (2.8%) (Central Electricity Authority (CEA), 2023). However, the installed capacity share of thermal based generation decreased through the years, from 63.3% in 2008–09 to 57% in 2022–23. Hydro-based generation has a capacity share of around 11.3%, whereas renewable based generation capacity has increased from 8.9% in 2008 to 30.1% in 2023 (CEA, 2023). Even though the installed capacity of renewable based generation has been growing, its gross generation is low due to a low utilisation factor.

The main players in the power generation sector can be categorised into three types based on ownership and operations. These are: (i) Central public sector undertakings, (ii) State public sector undertakings/State Electricity Boards, and (iii) Private sector companies.

The state sector held the majority of the power generation capacity until the early 2000s. But the Electricity Act of 2003 liberalised electricity production in India, leading to a licence free regime thereby creating a fresh competition in the generation sector, leading to a significant increase in the share of private companies involved in overall energy generation. During the period of 2008 to 2023, the share of the state sector in the total installed generation capacity declined from 54 to 25%, and the share of the central sector declined from 31 to 24%, whereas the share of the private sector increased significantly from 15 to 51% (CERC, 2023). The installed capacity of power generation by ownership in India in 2023 is presented in Fig. 1.

India's power generation witnessed its highest rate of growth in over 30 years in the financial year 2022–23. Power generation in India increased by 8.87% to 1,624.15 billion kilowatt-hours (kWh) in the financial year 2022–23 and India's power consumption stood at 130.57 BU in April 2023. The peak power demand in the country stood at 243.27 GW in November 2023 [4].

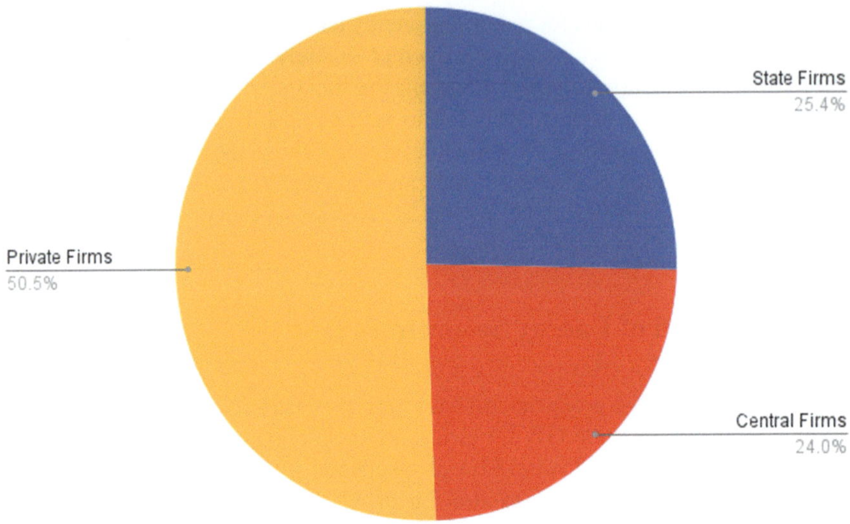

Fig. 1 Installed electricity generation capacity share by ownership in 2023. *Source* Central Electricity Authority (CEA), 2023

Even though India produces electricity from diverse sources, coal remains the most important and abundant source of energy in India, serving as the backbone for electricity production. India's consumption of coal has been increasing, reflecting the growing energy demands in the country. In 2023, coal consumption in India was around 777 million tonnes (MT), which is the second largest in the world behind China (Ministry of Coal, 2023). The country also ranks among the top coal producers, producing 893.19 million tonnes (MT) in the calendar year 2023 (Ministry of Coal, 2023). Even with its very high production of coal, India is the second largest coal importing country in the world. Among the total demand for the country's coal, almost 25% is met by coal imports, despite being the country with the 4th largest coal reserve in the world (Ministry of Coal, 2023).

Since the primary source of electricity generation in India is through thermal plants, the electricity generation sector accounts for the majority of total emissions in the country. The energy sector contributed about 75% of India's total emissions in 2019 (India Climate and Energy Dashboard (ICED), 2019). Among the top emitters, in 2022, China, the United States, and India increased their emissions compared to 2021, with India having the largest increase in relative terms (5%) (The Emissions Database for Global Atmospheric Research, 2023). As a country that aims to work to tackle climate change, it is necessary for India to control its emissions. Hence, it is important and relevant to analyse the efficiency of thermal power companies in India by also considering the emissions as an output in the production to study the emissions of the energy sector in India.

3 Literature Review

Studies have been carried out to evaluate the efficiency of power companies, and they are rather limited to developed countries. The studies that have analysed efficiency of power companies using a non—parametric method, namely, Data Envelopment Analysis (DEA) is reviewed here. Golany et al. (1994) used DEA analysis to examine the efficiency of power plants in Israel using data spanning seven years. The study revealed that most of the plants operated at decreasing return to scale and have a potential for improvement in terms of efficiency. Dia et al. [10] applied bootstrap DEA to evaluate the efficiency of 17 Canadian power generation companies over an 18 year period. The study indicated lower levels of overall technical and managerial efficiencies but relatively higher levels of scale efficiencies for the Canadian power generation companies. Shermeh et al. (2018) used Slack-Based Model (SBM) DEA to evaluate the efficiency of power companies in Iran. The study used 16 regional power companies to find the efficiency of each division of the power sector, such as generation, transmission, and distribution. The study found the transmission sector to be more efficient than other sectors. Navarro-Chávez et al. [14] investigated the efficiency of the electrical sector in Mexico between 2008 and 2015 by employing a DEA network model. Firstly, a factorial analysis is performed to identify latent dimensions, which are subsequently categorised into processes: generation, transmission, distribution, and sales. The DEA network model is then organised, with inputs and outputs specified for each node. The study found that transmission was identified as the most efficient node and only two of the thirteen regions were efficient, and other regions had scope for expansion. Sánchez-Ortiz et al. [17] assessed the effectiveness of distribution companies in the Spanish electrical industry for the period 2006–2015 and examined how overcapacity and tariff deficits impact their performance using DEA. The results indicated that excess capacity and tariff deficits had adverse effects on the Spanish electrical industry.

One of the major causes of concern for power generation companies is the emission of hazardous gas, which causes lots of environmental and medical threats. Subsequently, studies have also considered these undesirable outputs, like emissions in the form of NO_x, SO_x, CO_2, etc. as an additional output. Mahmoudi et al. [12] assessed the efficiency of thermal power plants while taking into account the generation of CO_2 emissions, which is an unwanted output. The study evaluated the effectiveness of thermal power plants taking into account their operational efficiency and environmental sustainability and concluded that the majority of Iranian thermal power plants are inefficient in their performance, causing economic, social, and environmental challenges. Chai et al. [7] used SBM-DEA model with undesirable output, like SO_x, NO_x, and soot emissions, to look at improvements in technical efficiency of China's thermal powers sector and how they related to industry indicators like the price-earnings ratio (P/E ratio). The study found that the overall efficiency of thermal power plants in China increased from 2017 to 2018.

However, studies on analysing the efficiency of the power sector in India in particular are rather scanty. Behera et al. [2] focused on assessing the efficiency of coal-fired power plants in India using DEA. The study found that 49 out of the 370 Decision Making Units (DMUs) analysed are deemed efficient. The study used total coal consumption, capital cost of the plants, maintenance expenditure, and the amount of electricity consumed as the key inputs, while power generated was the sole output. The study could not take account of uncontrolled environmental variables such as air emissions.

Although there have not been many studies using DEA in the power generation sector in India, studies have analysed the efficiency of the electricity distribution sector in India. Bobde et al. [3] estimated the efficiency of electricity distribution utilities in India for the period 2005–2012. They used a bootstrap estimation technique to conduct a two-stage DEA on 13 utilities in Maharashtra, Gujarat, and Delhi. The inputs used were number of employees, distribution line length, transformer capacity, and total assets and outputs accounted as number of customers and total electricity delivered. The study ranked the distribution companies (DISCOMs) using IRP, TOPSIS, and the Malmquist Index, which provided different perspectives on efficiency. Patyal et al. [15] assessed efficiency of 48 electricity DISCOMs across 24 states in India from 2015–16 to 2018–19. The study used multiple inputs like gross input energy, employee cost, Average Cost of Supply (ACS)-Average Revenue Realised (ARR) based on received subsidies, Aggregate Technical and Commercial AT&C losses, power purchase cost, and total borrowing. The outputs considered were gross energy sold, total revenue, and profit after tax, for assessing efficiency. The study utilised an integrated DEA-IRP-TOPSIS technique to categorise DISCOMs into efficient and inefficient segments and provided information for policymakers and industry experts in the DISCOMs. The study found that while there are efficient DISCOMs, there is room for improvement in the sector as a whole to enhance efficiency and sustainability. In a recent study, [9] evaluated the business performance of 10 power companies in India by incorporating both economic and social aspects using the DEA method and financial ratios. This study ranked the DMUs based on their efficiency scores and Return on Total Assets (ROTA) criterion.

The available studies show that most of the studies are confined to power plants and DISCOMS and are carried out in developed countries. The available evidence also indicates that very few studies are carried out in the Indian context and there is no evidence of modelling the data using undesirable output like emissions. This study is a modest attempt to fill this gap by addressing the research question of whether the thermal power generation companies in India utilise their scarce resources effectively to produce the power as well as whether they are efficient in terms of reducing emission of sulphur dioxide. The study also makes an attempt to evaluate whether the existing thermal power plants have scope for expansion or whether they have exhausted their scale of operations. The paper next proceeds to specify the data, methodology, and models used for empirical estimation.

4 Data, Methodology and Model Specification

The data used in the study is briefed in the following subsection.

4.1 Data

The present study utilises data about six prominent private thermal power companies that generate electricity in India. The data was collected from the annual reports of each company for the financial year 2022–2023. A non-parametric method, namely, Data Envelopment Analysis (DEA) is used to estimate efficiency of the firms. The following subsection details the technique.

4.2 Data Envelopment Analysis (DEA)

Data Envelopment Analysis (DEA) is one of the most widely recognized non-parametric linear programming method, developed by Charnes and Cooper in 1985, to evaluate the relative efficiency of similar Decision Making Units (DMUs). It is considered that these DMUs consume inputs, which are resources, and produce outputs, which are products and/or services. Furthermore, by using this technique, benchmarking for inefficient DMUs can be carried out without establishing a prior relationship between the inputs and outputs. The DEA establishes an efficiency frontier by assessing the effectiveness of all DMUs in relation to that frontier. An efficient DMU is one that is situated at the frontier and cannot be outperformed by any other DMU in terms of producing more outputs with an equal or smaller amount of input or using fewer inputs to generate an equal or higher number of outputs (Lovell 1993; Fare et al. 1994).

The conventional DEA are classified into input oriented and output oriented models. Charles, Cooper, and Rhodes in 1978 introduced an input oriented model with a constant return to scale (CRS) assumption to evaluate efficiency. Subsequently, in 1984, Banker, Charnes, Cooper proposed a Variable Constant to Scale (VRS) model. This approach is very widely used to deal with multi-input and multi-output problems.

The basic formulation of the input-oriented DEA model involves solving a linear programming problem. The objective is to maximise the efficiency score, subject to the constraint that the efficiency scores of all DMUs are less than or equal to one relative to the reference DMU. This input-oriented DEA can be represented mathematically as:

$$\text{Maximise} \frac{\sum_{j=1}^{n} \lambda_j x_{0j}}{\sum_{j=1}^{n} \lambda_j x_{ij}}$$

$$\text{Subject} \sum_{j=1}^{n} \lambda_j w_{ij} \leq x_{0i} \text{ for all i} = 1, 2, ..., \text{m}$$

where:

- Efficiency represents the efficiency score of the DMU being evaluated.
- Output_j and input_i denote the amount of the j-th output and i-th input, respectively.
- w_j and v_i are the weights assigned to the j-th outputs and inputs,respectively.
- λ is a scaling factor ensuring that the efficiency score is less than or equal to 1.

DEA assumes linearity, meaning inputs and outputs can be linearly combined through a weighted sum to measure efficiency. Moreover, DEA assumes the existence of an efficiency frontier, which acts as a benchmark and represents the highest output that can be produced from a particular input set. The methodology also assumes that the DMUs make decisions independently, ensuring that their efficiency is determined solely based on their own performance.

The study used the DEA software called DEAP 1.4.1, developed at the Computer Vision and Systems Laboratory (CVSL) at Université Laval in Quebec City, Canada, to assess the efficiency of the DMUs.

4.3 Model Specification

The study estimates the efficiency of thermal-based major private power companies in India for the time period 2022–23 using DEA. The profile of the sample of companies used in the analysis is shown in Table 1.

It may be noted from Table 1 that firm in the public sector (NTPC) contribute a relatively larger share of production and considering the large production scale and differences between private sector companies in terms of production scale and capacity with those of the public sector, only private companies are used for analysis in the study. However, the private sector produced almost 36.4% of the total electricity production in India, while the public sector, consisting of both the central and state sectors, contributed to the rest of the 63.6% of electricity in the year 2022 [4]. It may also be noted that the private sector produced around 32.6% of the total thermal energy in India. The relatively larger role of private companies in energy supply in India is very evident from Table 1 which shows the annual production in 2023. Table 1 shows that the private companies have varying production levels, and Adani Group and Tata Power are the ones with the largest level of production.

An input-oriented multi-stage DEA method is used to find the technical and scale efficiency of the private power companies and inputs and outputs used are described in Table 2.

The study follows multiple inputs consisting of the number of employees in the firm, installed capacity of the firm, and capital expenditure in alternate models. The outputs comprise of total revenue, total power generated and the inclusion of sulphur

Table 1 Company profile of selected power generation firms in India, 2023

Company	Year formed	Types of production	Installed capacity (MW)	Power generated in 2022–23 (MU)	Percentage of total power production
Adani Power	1996	Thermal, solar, and wind	12,450	53,510	3.294
JSW Energy	1994	Thermal, solar, hydro and wind	4559	23,485	1.44
Reliance Power	1995	Thermal, solar, hydro and wind	5945	37,379	2.301
Tata Power	1915	Thermal, solar, hydro and wind	14,110	54,052	3.33
Torrent Power	1996	Thermal, solar, natural gas and wind	4160	6218	0.383
Calcutta Electric Supply Corporation (CESC) Ltd	1978	Thermal, Solar, Natural Gas and Wind	2125	10,185	0.627
National Thermal Power Corporation (NTPC)*	1975	Thermal, solar, hydro and wind	72,254	399,000	24.56

* *Note* NTPC is the largest power generating firm and a public company, and is added to the table only as a reference
Source Annual Report of the Companies 2022–23; Power Sector at a Glance 2023, CEA

Table 2 Brief description of the inputs and outputs

Variable	Description
Inputs	
No. of employees	Total number of permanent employees in the company in a year
Capital expenditure	Total assets in terms of plants, property and equipment in crores
Outputs	
Total power generated	Total power generated by the company across plants in Million Units (MU)
Total revenue	Total income from all the operations in crore Rupees
SO_x emissions	Total amount of sulphur dioxide emitted by the plant in MT

dioxide emissions, which is an undesirable input. We adopt a method of reciprocal transformation to transform the values of the undesirable outputs into a form that can be used in the efficiency analysis. This transformation maintains the linear structure of the DEA model. The empirical estimates are presented next.

5 Empirical Estimates of Efficiency Scores

The study estimates how effectively the private thermal power companies in India allocate their resources to produce the given output. This is estimated by calculating technical and scale efficiency. Technical efficiency is defined as the ability of decision making units (DMU) to maximize outputs from a given set of inputs. It measures how well a DMU utilizes its resources compared to the best-performing DMUs. On the other hand, scale efficiency measures whether a DMU is operating at an optimal size. It examines whether the DMU could achieve more outputs by scaling up or down its operations.

The study employs two alternate models to estimate efficiency of the power firms. The model 1 uses the expenses of the firms breaking into recurring and non-recurring expenditure as inputs and takes total production of power as the output. However, power companies in India are challenged with distribution and transmission losses and also thermal companies emit pollutants that degrade the environment. Hence the study has considered an alternate model by keeping the inputs same as model 1 but the output captures the total revenue instead of production which also indirectly captures the loss of energy through transmission and distribution. Additionally, the sulphur dioxide emissions of these firms are also included as an output which is an undesirable output. The efficiency scores of the companies are estimated and presented in Table 3.

The Model 1 estimates show that overall, private power companies in India are only 64% technical efficient and have very weak scale efficiency (44%). It may be noted that Reliance Power is the only company which is technical and scale efficient in terms of model 1 while Adani Power is only technical efficient. The Adani and Tata Power which have the largest installed capacity have exhausted their economies and are operating on decreasing returns to scale.

However, when an alternate model is used including undesirable output SO_2 and total revenue earned by the firms, the overall technical efficiency score dropped to 61% and that of scale efficiency improved to 83%. The fall in technical efficiency may be because total revenue in comparison to total power generated might account for transmission and distribution loss of power which needs further academic scrutiny. It is interesting to note that Reliance Power is found efficient in model 2 as well.

It may be noted that Tata Power, one of the pioneering companies in the sector, has the highest number of employees, which is almost twenty times that of Reliance Power and 8 times that of Adani Power. This may increase the recurring expenses

Table 3 Estimates of technical and scale efficiency of private power firms in India 2023

Model 1				
Inputs: Number of employees, capital expenditure				
Outputs: Total power generated				
Company	Technical efficiency (CRS)	Technical efficiency (VRS)	Scale efficiency	Return to scale
Adani Power Ltd	0.528	1	0.528	DRS
JSW Energy	0.355	0.565	0.628	IRS
Reliance Power	1	1	1	-
Tata Power	0.087	1	0.087	DRS
Torrent Power	0.013	0.080	0.166	IRS
CESC Ltd	0.055	0.202	0.272	IRS
Mean technical efficiency: 0.641				
Mean scale efficiency: 0.447				
Model 2				
Inputs: Number of employees, capital expenditure				
Outputs: Total revenue, SO_x emission				
Company	Technical efficiency (CRS)	Technical efficiency (VRS)	Scale efficiency	Return to scale
Adani Power Ltd	0.207	0.369	0.562	IRS
JSW Energy	1	1	1	–
Reliance Power	1	1	1	–
Tata Power	0.08	0.098	0.817	DRS
Torrent Power	0.651	1	0.651	DRS
CESC Ltd	0.221	0.231	0.957	IRS
Mean technical efficiency: 0.616				
Mean scale efficiency: 0.831				

of the firm, which in turn pulls down its technical efficiency. The study is limited to the availability of data and further calls for extended analysis over a time series data and also estimates total factor productivity of these firms.

6 Conclusion

India's power sector heavily depends on thermal based power generation, contributing almost 74% of total generation in 2022–23 [4] and the private sector has been continuously investing and expanding its power generation capacity through the years to compete with the public sector. Also, as a fast developing nation, India focuses on decreasing its carbon footprint and emissions in order to achieve their target of net zero emission by 2070. Hence, it is important to study the efficiency of these private power companies by including undesirable outputs such as emissions.

The study uses DEA to estimate the technical and scale efficiency of six of the largest private power generating companies in India to assess how effectively these companies are utilising their scarce resources. An input-oriented multi-stage DEA on two models comprising expenditure of the firm as inputs and total production, total revenue and sulphur emissions as outputs, and the results indicated that the Indian power sector exhibits 61–64% efficiency and has a huge scope for improvement. Reliance is found to be the most efficient firm among them in all two models which may be due to the very low number of employees, indicating low recurring expenses and very low capital expenditure, thus helping the firm produce enough output with relatively less inputs. It is also found that Adani Power and Tata Power have the highest installed capacity, but are not efficient in production and Tata has the largest number of employees which increases their recurring expenditure.

This study contributes to the existing literature on the Indian power generation sector by incorporating undesirable output into the efficiency evaluation of private power companies thus by doing an evaluation framework to include the environmental impact as well. This study has limitations as it considers only limited time period of the study and non-availability of firm level data on emissions and energy losses. Future studies should consider integrating more recent data to understand how this industry has changed over time.

References

1. Adani Power Limited. Annual Report 2022–23. https://www.adanipower.com/-/media/Project/Power/Investors/Investors-Downloads/Annual-Reports/APL-2023.pdf
2. Behera SK, Dash AP, Farooquie JA (2015) Performance analysis of coal fired power plants in India. SSRN Electron J. https://doi.org/10.2139/ssrn.2694154
3. Bobde SM, Tanaka M (2018) Efficiency evaluation of electricity distribution utilities in India: a two-stage DEA with bootstrap estimation. J Oper Res Soc 69(9):1423–1434. https://doi.org/10.1080/01605682.2017.1398202
4. Central Electricity Authority-CEA (2023) All India electricity statistics general review 2023. https://cea.nic.in/wp-content/uploads/general/2022/GR_Final.pdf
5. Central Electricity Regulatory Commission (2023) Report on short-term power market in India 2022–23. https://cercind.gov.in/2023/market_monitoring/Annual%20Report%202022-23.pdf
6. CESC Limited. Annual Report 2022–23. https://www.cesc.co.in/storage/uploads/annreport/Annual%20Report_CESC_2022-23.pdf
7. Chai J, Fan W, Han J (2020) Does the Energy efficiency of power companies affect their industry status? A DEA analysis of listed companies in thermal power sector. Sustainability (Switzerland) 12(1). https://doi.org/10.3390/SU12010138
8. Chateau J, Dang G, Macdonald M, Spray J, Thube S (2023) A framework for climate change mitigation in India, WP/23/218, October 2023. https://www.imf.org/en/Publications/WP/Issues/2023/10/20/A-Framework-for-Climate-Change-Mitigation-in-India-535854
9. Chhillar I (2023) DEA and financial ratio analysis: efficiency of power plants in India-shareholder's view. Int J Financ Insur Risk Manag XIII(Issue 1)

10. Dia M, Shahi SK, Zéphyr L (2021) An assessment of the efficiency of Canadian power generation companies with bootstrap DEA. J Risk Financ Manag 14(10). https://doi.org/10.3390/jrfm14100498
11. JSW Energy. Annual Report 2022–23. https://www.jsw.in/sites/default/files/assets/downloads/energy/Financial%20Releases/Annual%20Reports/JSW%20Energy%20Limited%20Integrated%20Annual%20Report%202023.pdf
12. Mahmoudi R, Emrouznejad A, Khosroshahi H, Khashei M, Rajabi P (2019) Performance evaluation of thermal power plants considering CO_2 emission: a multistage PCA, clustering, game theory and data envelopment analysis. J Clean Prod 223:641–650. https://doi.org/10.1016/j.jclepro.2019.03.047
13. Ministry of Statistics and Programme Implementation (2023) Energy India statistics 2023. https://www.mospi.gov.in/sites/default/files/publication_reports/Energy_Statistics_2023/EnergyStatisticsIndia2023.pdf
14. Navarro-Chávez CL, Delfín-Ortega OV, Díaz-Pulido A (2020) Efficiency of the electricity sector in Mexico 2008–2015: an application of the DEA network model. Int J Energy Sect Manag 14(4):683–706. https://doi.org/10.1108/IJESM-03-2019-0019
15. Patyal VS, Kumar R, Lamba K, Maheshwari S (2023) Performance evaluation of Indian electricity distribution companies: an integrated DEA-IRP-TOPSIS approach. Energy Econ 124. https://doi.org/10.1016/j.eneco.2023.106796
16. Reliance Power. Annual Report 2022–23. https://www.reliancepower.co.in/documents/2181716/13074024/Annual_Report_2022_23.pdf
17. Sánchez-Ortiz J, Garcia-Valderrama T, Rodríguez-Cornejo V, Cabrera-Monroy F (2020) DEA window analysis and Malmquist index to assess efficiency and productivity in the Spanish electricity sector. Int J Energy Sect Manage 15(4):765–788. https://doi.org/10.1108/IJESM-03-2019-0020
18. Tata Power. Annual Report 2022–23. https://www.tatapower.com/pdf/investor-relations/104Annual-Report-2022-23.pdf
19. Torrent Power. Annual Report 2022–23. https://www.torrentpower.com/pdf/investors/AnnualReport_20230714192633.pdf

Modeling and Analysis of Pulsed Electric Field Treatment Chambers for Liquid Food Processing

Gajula Chandanasree, Thomas Mohan, and K. J. Suja

Abstract Pulsed Electric Field (PEF) processing is a promising technology for food preservation. Compared to thermal processing methods, PEF processing offers advantages like reduction in food processing time and energy consumption, higher retention of nutritional components, and better preservation of fresh flavour. However, the design of PEF treatment chambers and the optimization of operating parameters like intensity of the electric field, pulse duration, and flow rate are critical for achieving effective preservation while minimizing undesirable effects such as excessive heating or electrical breakdown. In static PEF processing, the geometry of the treatment chamber and the positioning of the electrodes need to be optimized to achieve uniform electric field distribution. Similarly, in continuous PEF processing, the configuration of the treatment chamber and the fluid velocity are important factors affecting the distribution of the electric field and resulting temperature distribution in the treated food. In the current work, after comparing some of the existing electrode configurations in treatment chambers, it was found that parallel plate treatment chambers are more efficient in providing a uniform electric field distribution. However, simulations of the continuous PEF treatment chamber containing parallel plate electrodes revealed that velocity of the liquid food inside different regions of the chamber was non-uniform, which leads to uneven levels of exposure to electric field. As a solution, this work proposes a semi-continuous mode of PEF treatment with parallel plate electrodes, which can provide a uniform level of treatment throughout the liquid food material.

G. Chandanasree (✉) · T. Mohan · K. J. Suja
Department of Electronics and Communication Engineering, National Institute of Technology Calicut, Calicut, India
e-mail: gchandanasree@gmail.com

T. Mohan
e-mail: thomas.mohan@mace.ac.in

K. J. Suja
e-mail: suja@nitc.ac.in

T. Mohan
Department of Electronics and Communication Engineering, Mar Athanasius College of Engineering, Kothamangalam, India

G. K. Rajanikant and P. Pré (eds.), *Perspectives on Global Transformation*, Lecture Notes in Electrical Engineering 1368, https://doi.org/10.1007/978-981-96-6707-9_12

Keywords Pulsed electric field · Liquid food processing · COMSOL Multiphysics software

1 Introduction

PEF involves applying high voltage [20–80 kV/cm] to the food placed between the electrodes in the form of short electric pulses. The treatment time required is less than a second and is suitable for preserving liquid and semi-liquid foods like juices, soups, eggs etc. The basic principle of PEF is electroporation, i.e., formation of pores on cell membranes under the effect of external electric field [1]. Depending upon the strength of the electric field applied, it may lead to reversible electroporation or irreversible electroporation [2] as illustrated in Fig. 1. For food processing applications, irreversible electroporation is required, so that successful microbial inactivation will occur. Hence, the PEF treatment system has to be designed such that the applied electric field is high enough so as to ensure irreversible electroporation.

1.1 PEF Treatment System

Typically, the PEF treatment system consists of a high-voltage pulsed power supply generator, at least one or more number of treatment chambers to transfer high-voltage electric pulses to the food, a control unit and a monitoring unit consisting of computer

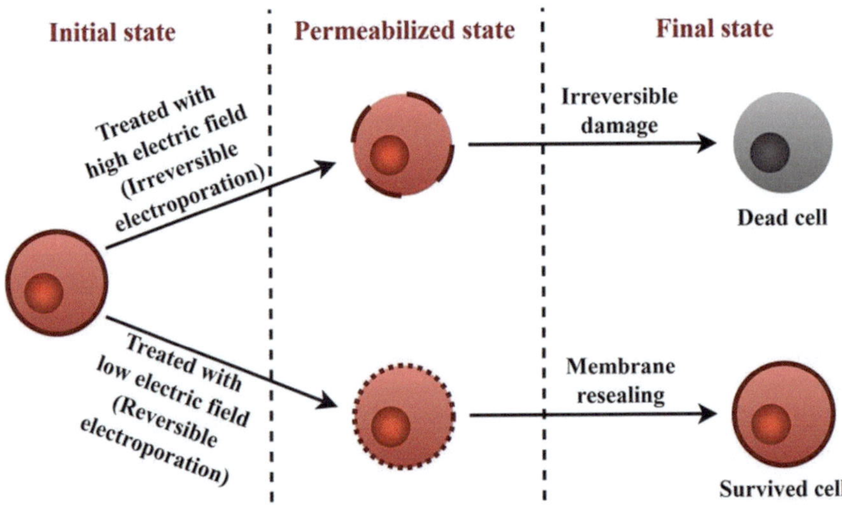

Fig. 1 Schematic illustration of electroporation on a single cell

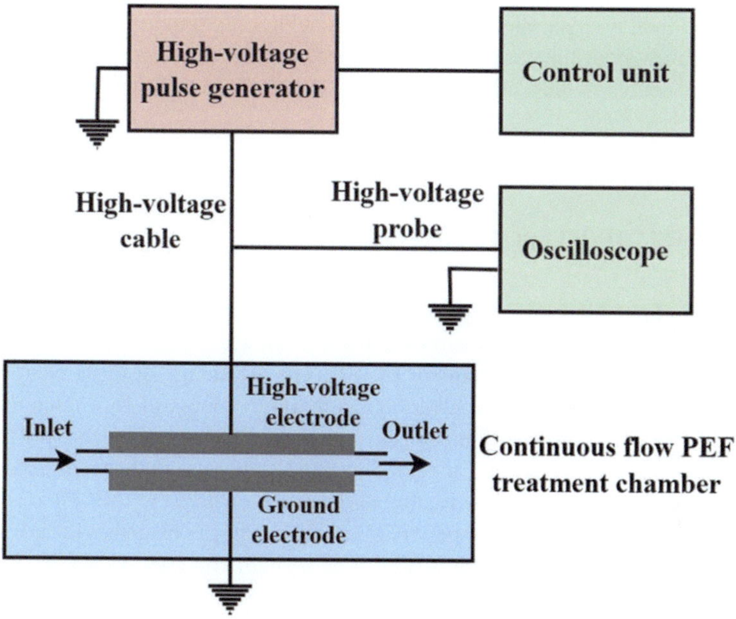

Fig. 2 PEF treatment system

and oscilloscope, to record voltage and current waveforms which are applied to the food. Figure 2 displays the block diagram of a sample PEF treatment system.

Treatment chambers can be static or continuous processing systems. It consists of one or more high voltage electrodes and ground electrodes and the treatment zone for fruit juice lies in between the electrodes. Treatment chambers should have uniform electric fields to subject all microorganisms in the juice to the same level of exposure. Proper care in designing the chamber is to be taken so that each unit volume of juice is subjected to the necessary number of pulses to bring about the inactivation of microbial cells.

The key features of PEF are (i) short treatment time of food (ii) the ability to preserve liquid foods and semi-liquid foods (iii) the ability to retain sensory properties like colour, flavour and nutrients [3–6]. Applications of PEF include the preservation of liquids like juices [4–6] and semi-solid foods like eggs [7], and extraction of oils and sugars [8, 9]. PEF processes have been found to be very effective in the preservation of solid and liquid food items which do not contain air bubbles.

In this work, some of the existing models of treatment chambers are compared. The comparison shows that the treatment chamber with parallel electrodes is better in providing a uniform electric field distribution. But, from the simulations of the continuous PEF treatment chamber with parallel plate electrodes, it is noticed that the velocity of the liquid food inside different regions of the chamber is different, which can lead to uneven levels of exposure to electric field and inconsistent microbial inactivation. As a feasible solution, this work proposes a semi-continuous mode of PEF treatment with parallel plate electrodes, which can provide a uniform level of treatment throughout the chamber. The proposed system can provide more consistency in the levels of microbial inactivation during PEF treatment of liquid food materials.

2 Existing Models of Treatment Chamber

Many works have focused on development of different designs for PEF treatment chambers. There are static treatment chambers, where the fruit juice does no undergo motion during electric field treatment [8, 10]. The advantage of these chambers is the simplicity in design. The disadvantage is that the amount of fruit juice that can be treated in one batch is limited by the volume of the chamber and continuous human intervention is required for reloading the batch. Some other research works have focused on continuous flow treatment chambers, where the fruit juice is under constant motion during PEF treatment [11–14]. This type of design has the advantage that more amount of juice can be treated with a small chamber. However, in these designs, the velocity of fruit juice inside the chamber is a vital factor that decides the level of exposure to electric field, which makes their design more complex.

2.1 COMSOL Simulation of Treatment Chambers

The software tool that is used for all the simulations in the current study is COMSOL Multiphysics. For modelling the electric field distribution, Electrostatics module in COMSOL was used and for fluid dynamics, Laminar Flow module was used.

Governing equations for electrostatic module. Electrostatics module, uses Eqs. (1) and (2) to calculate the field strength.

$$\nabla \cdot (\varepsilon_0 \varepsilon_r \boldsymbol{E}) = \rho_v \tag{1}$$

$$\boldsymbol{E} = -\nabla V \tag{2}$$

where $\boldsymbol{E}$ is the electric field strength, ε_0 and ε_r are the free space permittivity and relative permittivity of medium respectively, ρ_v is the volume charge density, and V is the electric potential. At the outer boundary of the model, normal components of the electric field are assumed to be zero. Also, initial value of electric potential of all the components at time $t = 0$ are assumed to be zero.

Governing equations for laminar flow module. The laminar flow module uses Navier–Stokes equations which are given in Eqs. (3) and (4).

$$\rho\frac{\partial \boldsymbol{u}}{\partial t} + \rho(\boldsymbol{u}.\nabla)\boldsymbol{u} = \nabla.\left[-p\boldsymbol{I} + \mu\left(\nabla\boldsymbol{u} + (\nabla\boldsymbol{u})^T\right)\right] + \boldsymbol{F} \tag{3}$$

$$\nabla.(\rho\boldsymbol{u}) = 0 \tag{4}$$

where the parameters of the equation are fluid density ρ, fluid velocity $\boldsymbol{u}$, time t, fluid pressure p, identity matrix $\boldsymbol{I}$, dynamic viscosity μ, and body force density $\boldsymbol{F}$. At the boundary, the wall of the chamber is defined to be non-slipping and the initial values of fluid velocity and pressure at time t = 0 are assumed to be zero.

Meshing. To ensure correct results from the simulation, the geometries of the treatment chambers were meshed using the "Extremely Fine" mesh setting. This ensured that the resolution was high enough to accommodate even the sharper edges in the chamber geometry.

2.2 *Common Chamber Designs*

Some common designs of chamber used for PEF treatment are parallel plate, coaxial, and co-linear designs. Simulation of electric field distribution in these three geometries were done using COMSOL Multiphysics software. In all the simulated cases, the fruit juice is placed between the two electrodes of the treatment chamber. Relative permittivity of fruit juice was set as 70 and the conductivity was set as 0.25 S/m in all the simulated scenarios. A 20 kV potential was applied to the high-voltage electrode and the other was grounded.

Several works have reported successful microbial inactivation with a PEF treatment time of around 150 μs [5, 15]. The treatment time can be calculated using the Eq. (5) as given in [16].

$$t = \frac{V_{chamber}}{F} f\tau \tag{5}$$

where $V_{chamber}$ is the volume of the chamber (m^3), F is the flow rate (m^3/s), f is the pulse repetition rate (Hz) and τ is the pulse width (s). Considering a sample PEF treatment scenario where pulses of width 15 μs and pulse repetition rate of 1 Hz are applied to a treatment chamber of volume 1 L with an inlet pipe of diameter 1 cm, in order to achieve a treatment time of 150 μs, the fluid has to be pumped at a velocity of 1.27 m/s. Hence, to ensure that the fluid gets sufficient treatment time, it was decided to use a lower fluid velocity of 1 m/s for all the simulations.

Parallel plate treatment chamber. As the name suggests, this chamber consists of two parallel plates [17] as shown in Fig. 3. Continuous fluid flow mechanism has been implemented inside the chamber with the juice velocity set as 1 m/s. Electric Field and juice velocity distribution inside this chamber is shown in Fig. 4. Even though we can observe a uniform electric field and velocity across most of the treatment zone,

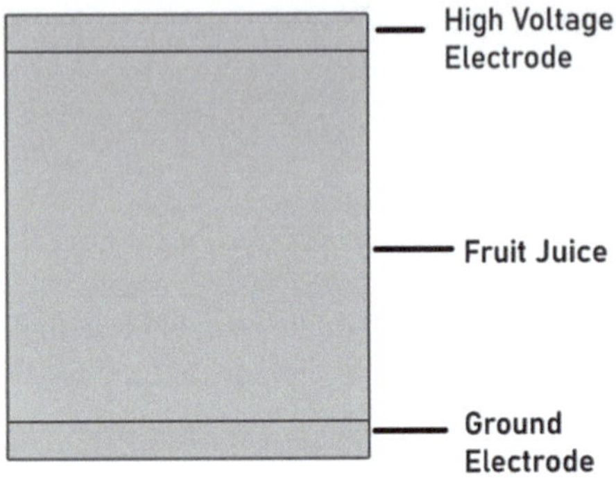

Fig. 3 Parallel plate treatment chamber

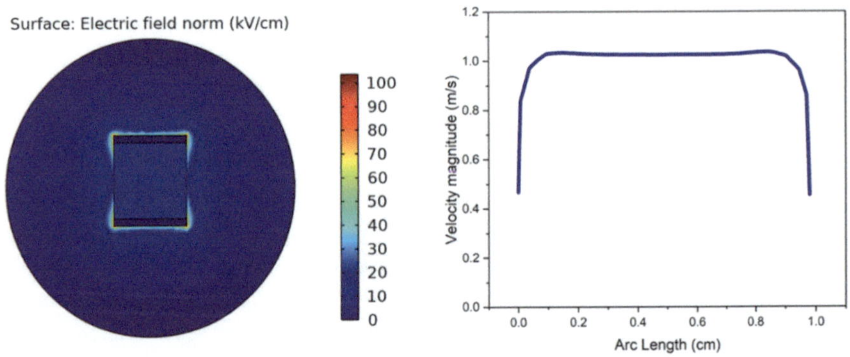

Fig. 4 Electric field and fluid velocity inside parallel plate chamber

higher electric fields are seen near the sharp edges of both the electrodes. This results in more energy dissipation near the edges of the electrodes. In Fig. 4, the velocity of the fruit juice along an imaginary line drawn horizontally across the centre of the chamber is plotted.

Co-axial treatment chamber. It consists of two concentric cylindrical electrodes [18]. Here, the inner electrode is high voltage electrode and other is ground electrode. These electrodes are placed in an acrylic container. Here, the juice is made to flow through a cavity inside the high voltage electrode and made to flow at velocity 1 m/s. Electric field along a horizontal line across the space between the two electrodes is plotted in Fig. 5. It is clear that the intensity of electric field is non-uniform across the treatment zone.

Co-linear treatment chamber. A co-linear treatment chamber has electrodes kept side by side along an axis [19]. The high-voltage and ground electrodes are placed alternatively as in Fig. 6. Between the electrodes, insulators are placed. Single-unit or multi-unit treatment chambers can be implemented in this way.

As shown in Fig. 6a, the treatment zone i.e., the gap between the electrodes, is much shorter for a single unit chamber, which reduces the treatment time. So multiple units of co-linear treatment chambers are connected in series which results

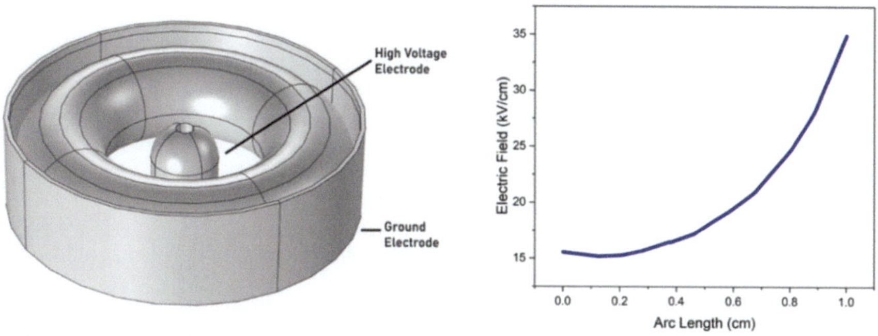

Fig. 5 Co-axial chamber and electric field distribution

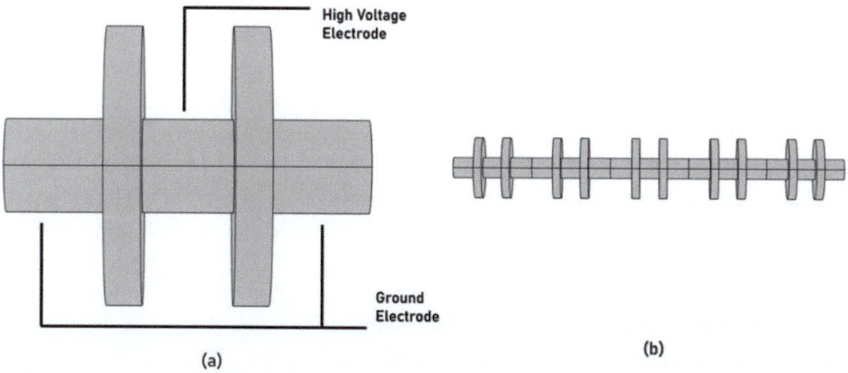

Fig. 6 **a** Co-linear treatment chamber, **b** series of co-linear chambers

in the increase of treatment time. Here, in Fig. 6b, five chambers are connected. The field distribution across the axis of the chamber is shown in Fig. 7. Electric field is observed in the treatment zone. Fruit juice, after getting treated in one unit of the chamber, gets some time to cool down before passing to the next unit, thus preventing the heating up of the juice. Exposure to electric field inside multiple units of chambers results in better inactivation of microorganisms.

2.3 *Effect of Insulator Layer Over Electrodes*

Insulators play a crucial role in the treatment chambers. In addition to providing electrical insulation, these insulators ensure that the electrical energy is properly contained within the treatment chamber, thus preventing leakage or dissipation into the surrounding environment. An electrode covered with an insulator produces a different electric field distribution pattern compared to an uninsulated electrode. To

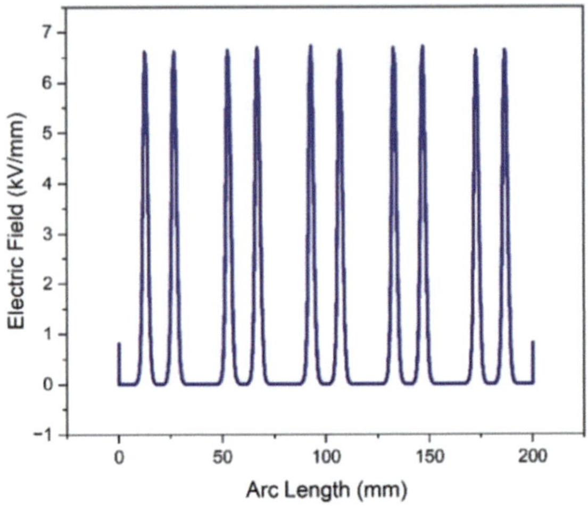

Fig. 7 Electric field inside a series co-linear chamber

study this effect, the high voltage electrode of the parallel plate chamber was covered with an insulator and its field distribution was analyzed. The thickness of the insulator was varied and the respective electric field intensities at the midpoint of the treatment zone are plotted in Fig. 8. It was determined that electric field is decreased with an increase in insulator thickness.

From all the above simulations, it can be inferred that among the three configurations, parallel plate and co-linear treatment chambers have uniform field distribution and co-axial has non-uniform distribution of electric field. However, the co-linear chamber is more complex in design compared to the parallel plate chamber. We also observed that the usage of insulator layer reduces the electric field intensity in the treatment chamber. Hence, the high electric field intensity observed near the sharp edges of electrodes in a parallel plate chamber can be reduced using an insulator.

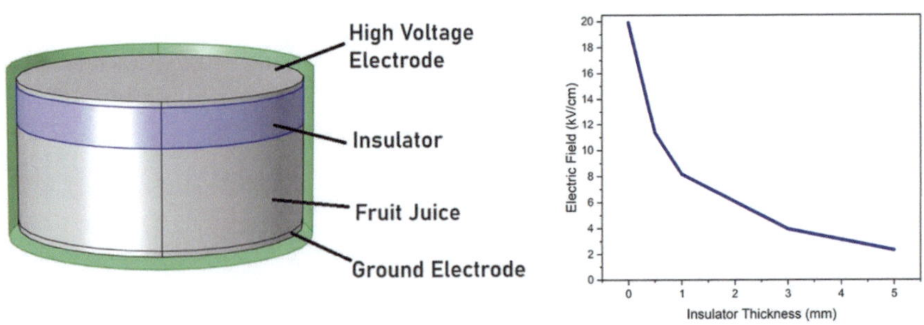

Fig. 8 Electric field versus insulator thickness in parallel plate treatment chamber

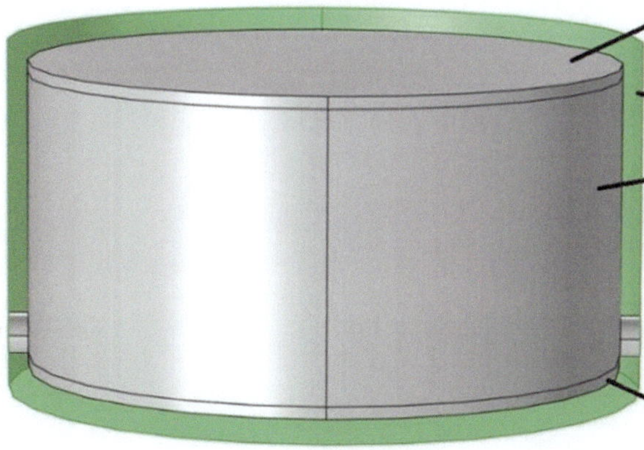

Fig. 9 Parallel plate continuous flow treatment chamber

3 Proposed Model

After observing the advantages and limitations of all the previous chambers, a parallel plate treatment chamber with continuous flow mechanism was proposed. The chamber, as shown in Fig. 9, has a cylindrical shape with a diameter of 15 cm and a height of 7 cm. Inlet and outlet valves are provides to enable continuous flow of juice through the chamber.

The electrodes in this chamber are made up of brass and the whole setup is enclosed in acrylic. The outer acrylic covering reduces the high electric field intensity produced outside the chamber due to the sharp edges of the electrodes, as can be seen in Fig. 10. The ground electrode is fixed, but the high voltage electrode can be moved vertically, which makes it possible to vary the electric field intensity inside the chamber. An electric potential of 20 kV was applied to the high voltage electrode and the 2D view of electric field is shown in Fig. 10.

Now, the distance between electrodes were varied and the resulting electric field was analysed. Variation of electric field depending upon the electrode gap is shown in Fig. 11. We can see that the electric field distribution is uniform across the chamber for a particular electrode gap and as the electrode gap increases, the electric field intensity decreases.

A uniform level of electric field exposure throughout the whole chamber can be ensured only if the velocity of fruit juice inside the chamber is constant. To analyse this, velocity of the juice at the chamber at different heights was plotted and the result is shown in Fig. 12.

It was observed that velocity is much more at the bottom of the chamber where inlet and outlet valves are situated. This non-uniform velocity results in non-uniform exposure to electric field. To tackle this issue, the continuous flow mode of the chamber was modified to semi-continuous mode. In this semi-continuous mode, a microcontroller-based system is used to control the inlet and outlet valves. A time

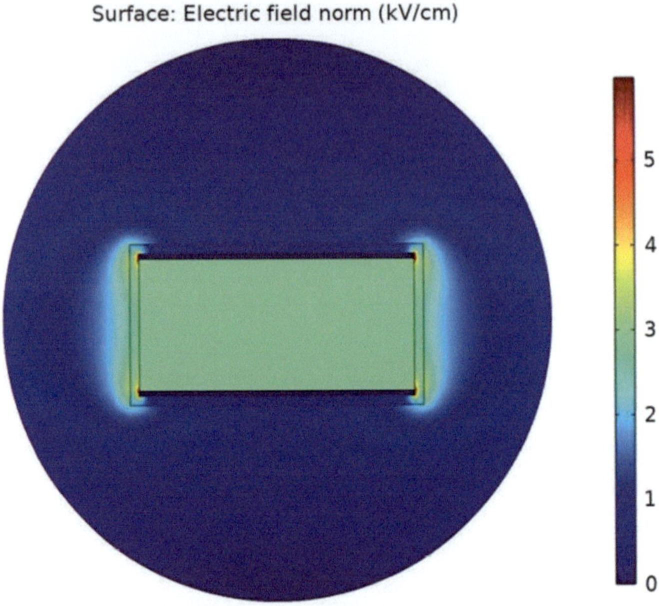

Fig. 10 Electric field for a parallel plate chamber with acrylic covering

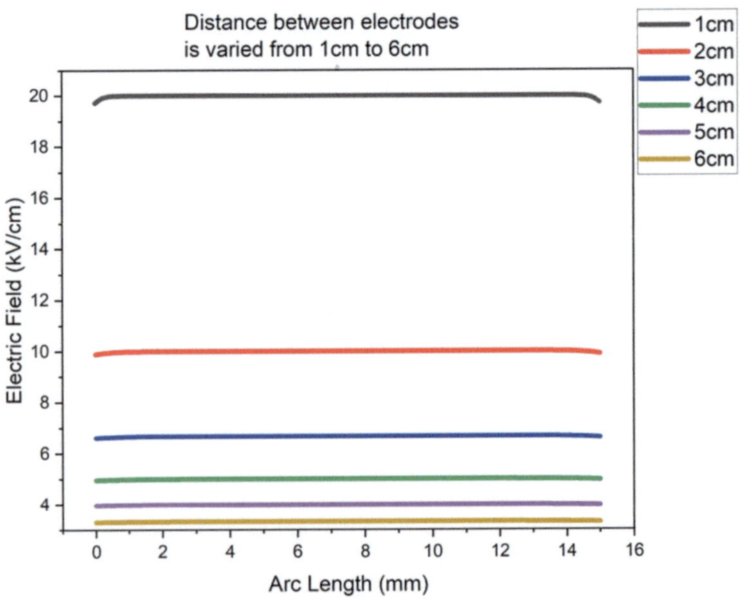

Fig. 11 Electric field when distance between electrodes is varied

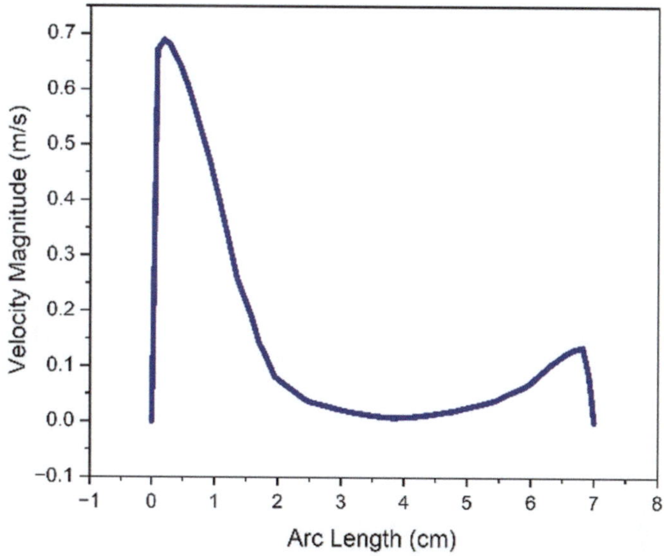

Fig. 12 Velocity distribution along the axis of the cylindrical chamber

duration-based implementation can be used to ensure that both the inlet and outlet valves are closed during the application of PEF. This will ensure that the velocity inside the chamber is kept constant. Once sufficient number of pulses are applied, the microcontroller can operate the inlet & outlet valves so as to take the treated fruit juice outside the chamber and fill the chamber with fresh juice for the next cycle of pulses.

4 Conclusions

Several Pulsed Electric Field treatment chamber models were compared. Every model has its own merits and demerits. Compared to co-axial treatment chamber, parallel plate and co-linear treatment chambers produce more uniform levels of electric field distribution. Static processing is easy to implement, but it is not generally preferred for bulk treatment as it is time-consuming and requires constant human intervention. Continuous flow treatment systems proved to be more efficient for bulk processing. However, in continuous processing, non-uniform velocity of the fruit juice inside the chamber causes non-uniform levels of microbial inactivation. After analysing all these factors, a semi-continuous flow-based treatment system was designed. It was shown that this new semi-continuous chamber provides a uniform level of exposure to electric field and is best suited for bulk PEF processing of fruit juice.

Acknowledgements The author(s) acknowledge that the access to COMSOL Multiphysics software used for this work was provided by I-STEM (Indian Science Technology and Engineering facilities Map), which is supported by the Office of the Principal Scientific Adviser to the Government of India.

References

1. Novac BM, Banakhr FA, Smith IR, Pecastaing L, Ruscassie R, De Ferron AS, Pignolet P (2013) Demonstration of a novel pulsed electric field technique generating neither conduction currents nor Joule effects. IEEE Trans Plasma Sci 42(1):216–228
2. Geboers B, Scheffer HJ, Graybill PM, Ruarus AH, Nieuwenhuizen S, Puijk RS, van den Tol PM, Davalos RV, Rubinsky B, de Gruijl TD, Miklavčič D, Meijerink MR (2020) High-voltage electrical pulses in oncology: irreversible electroporation, electrochemotherapy, gene electrotransfer, electrofusion, and electroimmunotherapy. Radiology 295(2):254–272
3. Arshad RN, Abdul-Malek Z, Munir A, Ahmad MH, Nawawi Z, Sidik MAB, Jumani TA, Khan I, Alotaibi H, Khan A (2021) An improved electroporator with continuous liquid flow and double-exponential waveform for liquid food pasteurization. IEEE Access 9:147732–147742
4. Kantala C, Supasin S, Intra P, Rattanadecho P (2022) Evaluation of pulsed electric field and conventional thermal processing for microbial inactivation in Thai orange juice. Foods 11(8):1102
5. Lee H, Choi S, Kim E, Kim YN, Lee J, Lee DU (2020) Effects of pulsed electric field and thermal treatments on microbial reduction, volatile composition, and sensory properties of orange juice, and their characterization by a principal component analysis. Appl Sci 11(1):186
6. Dziadek K, Kopeć A, Dróżdż T, Kiełbasa P, Ostafin M, Bulski K, Oziembłowski M (2019) Effect of pulsed electric field treatment on shelf life and nutritional value of apple juice. J Food Sci Technol 56:1184–1191
7. Agregán R, Munekata PE, Putnik P, Pateiro M, Bursać Kovačević D, Zavadlav S, Lorenzo JM (2023) The use of novel technologies in egg processing. Food Rev Intl 39(5):2854–2874
8. Barros M, Redondo L, Rego D, Serra C, Miloudi K (2022) Extraction of essential oils from plants by hydrodistillation with pulsed electric fields (PEF) pre-treatment. Appl Sci 12(16):8107
9. Delso C, Berzosa A, Sanz J, Álvarez I, Raso J (2022) Two-step PEF processing for enhancing the polyphenol concentration and decontaminating a red grape juice. Foods 11(4):621
10. Liu Z, Esveld E, Vincken JP, Bruins ME (2019) Pulsed electric field as an alternative pre-treatment for drying to enhance polyphenol extraction from fresh tea leaves. Food Bioprocess Technol 12:183–192
11. Araujo EJ, Lopes IJ, Ramirez JA (2021) Numerical study of treatment chambers for single and multi-stage pulsed electric field systems. IET Sci Meas Technol 15(4):385–397
12. Qin S, Li H, Wang R, Fan K, Huang S, Meng J (2023) Pulsed electric field inactivation of microorganism using chambers with different electrode topologies. IEEE Trans Plasma Sci 51(2):526–533
13. Rezaeimotlagh A, Serasinghe P, Asad AM, Trujillo FJ (2020) The effect of geometrical modifications on the performance of co-linear chambers for non-thermal radio frequency electric fields processing: a numerical study with experimental validation. Innov Food Sci Emerg Technol 64:102401
14. Wang Y, Sha K, Guo X, Chen J, Chen Q, Jiang F (2023) Optimization and simulation of pulsed electric field treatment chamber for food sterilization. Food Sci Technol 43:e126022
15. Huang K, Jiang T, Wang W, Gai L, Wang J (2014) A comparison of pulsed electric field resistance for three microorganisms with different biological factors in grape juice via numerical simulation. Food Bioprocess Technol 7:1981–1995

16. De Gol C, Moodycliffe A, den Besten HM, Zwietering MH, Beyrer M (2024) Pulsed electric field treatment for preservation of Chlorella suspensions and retention of gelling capacity. Food Res Int 182:114154
17. Masood H, Diao Y, Cullen PJ, Lee NA, Trujillo FJ (2018) A comparative study on the performance of three treatment chamber designs for radio frequency electric field processing. Comput Chem Eng 108:206–216
18. Shaker Y (2019) Modeling of pulsed electric field for liquid food processing using simulation methods. In: 2019 international conference on digitization (ICD). IEEE, pp 14–17
19. Matra K, Buppan P, Techaumnat B (2020) Analytical and experimental studies on the application of a series of treatment chambers for *Escherichia coli* inactivation by pulsed electric fields. Appl Sci 10(12):4071

MIX
Papier aus verantwortungsvollen Quellen
Paper from responsible sources
FSC® C105338
FSC
www.fsc.org

If you have any concerns about our products,
you can contact us on
ProductSafety@springernature.com

In case Publisher is established outside the EU,
the EU authorized representative is:
Springer Nature Customer Service Center GmbH
Europaplatz 3, 69115 Heidelberg, Germany

Printed by Libri Plureos GmbH
in Hamburg, Germany